INFORMAL MARRIAGE, COHABITATION
AND THE LAW 1750–1989

Also published by Stephen Parker
COHABITEES

Informal Marriage, Cohabitation and the Law 1750 – 1989

STEPHEN PARKER
Solicitor, Senior Lecturer in Law,
Australian National University

St. Martin's Press   New York

First published in the United States of America in 1990

Printed in Hong Kong

ISBN 0–312–03999–9

Library of Congress Cataloging-in-Publication Data
Parker, Stephen, LL.B.
Informal marriage, cohabitation, and the law, 1750 – 1989/ Stephen Parker.
p.   cm.
Includes bibliographical references.
ISBN 0–312–03999–9
1.Marriage law—Great Britain—History.   2.Unmarried couples—Legal
status, laws, etc.—Great Britain—History.   I.Title.
KD753.P37   1990
346.4201'6'09—dc20
[344.2061609]
                                                                        89–70030
                                                                        CIP

Contents

Acknowledgements

This book grew out of a doctoral thesis and I am grateful to the following, who read part or all of the thesis and who made helpful comments: Peter Alcock, Hugh Bevan, Stephen Bottomley, Harry Calvert, Bill Chambliss, Robert Dingwall, Rhian Ellis Parker and Pauline Todd. Particular thanks are due to Harry Calvert for encouragement and Rhian Ellis Parker for encouragement bordering on a campaign.

1 Introduction

1. AIMS

The concept of marriage is of central importance in many disciplines within the social sciences. Feminist concern with the family as a major site of women's oppression has targeted marriage as a crucial ideological and material institution (Smart, 1984, p. 144). Nuptiality has been the subject of much recent literature concerning the social history of the family, particularly within the demographic approach (Anderson, 1980, p. 18). In legal studies generally, and family law particularly, entry into marriage is seen naturally as immediately triggering rights and obligations between the parties themselves and also between them and third parties, such as children or the State. Yet despite its centrality to so much scholarship, marriage itself is infrequently problematised.

One illustration of this is the explanations offered by social historians for apparent fluctuations in illegitimacy rates. Laslett postulated the existence of a 'deviant subsociety of bastard bearers' (Laslett, 1977) whilst Shorter suggested a general ideological shift that unfroze the libido 'in the blast of the wish to be free' (Shorter, 1977). Neither dwelt on the point that whatever defines marriage will define non-marriage and consequently the legitimacy of children although Laslett and his colleagues in the Cambridge Group for the History of Population and Social Structure have subsequently adopted a more cautious tone. We are now told, in unappealing terms, that 'in certain cases it would appear that we are observing bastard-bearers who belong to families where the distinction between legal and illegal (*sic*) marriage remained uncertain' (Laslett, 1980, p. 134).

This book is about the way that the State, through its laws, has created and then adjusted the boundaries of legal marriage. It is not, however, intended to be a legal textook but more an attempt at explaining how certain laws have come about. Nor am I claiming that the State has a monopoly over the meaning of marriage. In fact, the latter part of the book specifically concerns the way that unmarried cohabitation is attracting legal consequences. The State most certainly does not *call* these relationships marriage. It does, on the other hand, increasingly regulate them *as if* they were marriage. In

1

summary, I am interested in how and why the law has created points
beyond which two people who are, or were, living together in a
domestic relationship become subject to legal consequences which
would not arise between them if there were no domestic relationship.
To put it slightly differently, why do some forms of cohabitation
become subject to legal regulation whilst others do not?

I argue that marriage is continually redefined through legal and
social practice. The account begins at a time when marriage could be
relatively formless and then traces the story through the high point of
formality and towards a retreat from formality as cohabitation is
increasingly juridified. In the course of exploring this I aim to suggest
ways in which changing economic, social and political circumstances
contribute to the process of redefining the dominant meaning of
marriage and, to a lesser extent, how the new meaning acts back on
those circumstances. The book is therefore more generally about the
relationship between economy, society and family law.

The material for the book derives largely from a doctoral thesis on
the history of informal marriage (Parker, 1985). That thesis in turn
was prompted by the material uncovered when writing a straightfor-
ward legal text on modern unmarried cohabitation (Parker, 1981 and
1987). When looking at the origins of the cohabitation rule in social
security law I discovered that cohabitation had been recognised in the
unemployment benefit legislation of the 1920s, initially for the
purpose of *increasing* the amount of benefit. In the course of the
parliamentary debates on the Unemployed Workers (Temporary
Provisions) Bill 1922 one labour MP suggested that 'it is only the
parson's fee that makes her a wife' (W. Thorne, Off. Debs. (HC) vol.
147, col. 1579). This prompted the idea of looking at the history of
the parson's fee. The resulting thesis attempted to demonstrate how
marriage laws over time have assimilated, or gathered in, relationships which approximate to the current form of legal marriage
and have attempted to deter those which do not.

2. SUMMARY

The year 1750 has been taken as a starting point for a number of
reasons. The simplest of these is that marriage law was transformed
by Lord Hardwicke's Marriage Act 1753 and it is essential to describe
the events leading up to the passage of the Act. Second, it shortly
predates what is still (not unproblematically) called the Industrial

Revolution and the formation of social classes along distinctively modern lines (Thompson, 1968: Malcolmson, 1981, p. 148). Third, at least one writer has suggested that it was the date when the modern family arose among the bourgeoisie in Europe (Poster, 1978, p. 167), although this view is not without its critics, particularly as regards England. Overall, however, 1750 should not be seen as an historical 'moment' and I will spend a little time in the next chapter describing marriage practices and laws going back several centuries earlier.

Chapter 2 takes a static view of society, family and marriage in the mid-eighteenth century. I describe at some length popular marriage customs and the extent to which they articulated with formal church and civil law. I also suggest ways in which marriage entry related to prevailing social and economic conditions, and try, so far as source material allows, to be conscious of class, gender, generation and religious distinctions. Whilst chapter 2 deals mainly with the practices of ordinary people, chapter 3 concerns marriage in the governing classes. It suggests why clandestine marriage became perceived as a social problem—although I venture that it was actually only so amongst the propertied classes—and why Lord Hardwicke's Act took the form it did.

Chapter 4 looks at the consequences of Lord Hardwicke's Act and the extent to which its requirements were compiled with. I chart the emerging pressure for civil marriage and examine the Marriage Act 1836 which permitted marriage in a register office and certain non-Anglican places of worship. The 1836 Act is the last major statutory reform to be discussed although the chapter also contains accounts of two more minor adjustments to the boundary; marriage to a deceased wife's sister and the brief legal life of the 'unmarried wife' in unemployment benefit legislation. After the 1836 Act, our attention begins to shift away from the clear legal boundary between formal marriage and other forms of relationship and turns towards a more blurred liminal status as some kinds of cohabitation are accorded legal consequences similar to those of formal marriage. In a simple sense, I look at the sharp rise and gradual fall of the significance of formal marriage as a trigger of legal rights and duties. The final part of the book covers the rapid growth in cohabitation law over the last two decades. The process is evaluated against the background of changing strategies in family law as a whole. In turn, family law is situated in the context of transformations within British society since 1945.

The tolerant reader may have suspended concern over the meanings I attach to certain words, bearing in mind that the above was only a brief summary. It is appropriate here, however, to talk about definitions; particularly that of marriage. Precise lanugage not only helps the reader in following the text it also reflects on the conceptual clarity of the writer. I have found it very difficult to come up with a typology of relationships ranging from the most formal orthodox marriage entry to the establishment of a consciously 'alternative' household. The difficulty in doing so actually illustrates a central theme of the book; that there is no monopoly over the meaning of marriage. The so-called tidy mind might prefer that 'marriage' is reserved for that which is incontrovertibly recognised by the law as marriage and that 'lesser' forms are ascribed other terms. The major problem with such an approach is that it ignores the subjective meanings with which people endow their relationships. My guess is that a considerable number of people who have not been through a legally recognised ceremony regard themselves as married. This was particularly true in the eighteenth century where local practices meant that many, if not most, adults in an area might not be recognised by the civil law as married. But it is also true of today. A solicitor in the north of England (where there is a long tradition of informal marriage) recently told me of being instructed by a client to obtain a divorce and it was only well into the interview that it turned out that there had been no formal marriage (and consequently no divorce was necessary).

The tidy mind might still object that people's views about the name of their relationship are irrelevant; people are either right or wrong. I regard the subjective meanings of the parties as important because we are not so much interested in words on a document but in the complex interplay between personal, social and legal practice. One theme which should emerge from the following chapters is that social meanings of marriage create pressure for the legal meaning to come into line, although I will argue that it is more complex than that. I prefer to say, at the risk of criticism from lawyers, that there is a variety of marriages within society. This has the consequence that modern 'cohabitation' should not necessarily be seen as deviancy which poses a threat to 'marriage'. It may, more accurately, simply be a revival of private ordering—of social marriage. Seen in this light, the interesting question is how law and State practice respond to and seek to structure new forms of relationship.

I am not alone in avoiding definitional issues. J.R. Gillis in his recent major work subtitled *British Marriages 1600 to the Present*

(Gillis, 1985) fails to define marriage itself and resorts to a distinction between official and unofficial marriages. Similarly, Alan Macfarlane's sweeping account of *Marriage and Love in England, 1300–1840* slides over the issue. In the chapter on courtship and wedding, he deals with betrothal and spousals, which will become relevant to our concerns. He simply says that the 'history and changing legal status of the betrothal is a subject of considerable complexity which merits longer treatment' and that by the sixteenth century the spousal had come to mean different things in different contexts (Macfarlane, 1986, p. 299).

I make use of three main terms. *Formal marriage* is that which before 1754 was regarded by church and civil authorities as sufficient to carry full religious and legal consequences. After 1753 it is that which complies fully with the provisions of statute law. It is simpler to use 'formal marriage' than 'legal marriage' because the latter term runs into difficulty when one considers relationships which have some marriage-like consequences in law. *Informal marriage* is that which before 1754 carried some religious and legal consequences. After Lord Hardwicke's Act, informal marriage became a purely private emulation of formal marriage, although often accompanied by community endorsement. *Cohabitation* is that which is not regarded either by the parties or the community as marriage-like. It refers to the factual circumstance of sharing the same household. These are, of course, ideal types to a certain extent. Whilst formal marriage is usually recognisable without difficulty, the distinction between informal marriage and cohabitation may be blurred, if only because the participants may have different perceptions of the relationship. The distinction becomes even harder to maintain in the modern period, particularly if the State imposes marriage-like consequences when either or both of the participants do not intend them. Furthermore, the notion of 'a household', which in this typology is the only requirement for cohabitation, involves something more than an address. As soon as one defines it further by reference to 'sharing' a new set of problems arises. Although it is in common parlance, I avoid 'common law marriage' because it now has a distinct legal meaning (basically it is a marriage in circumstances not reached by Lord Hardwicke's Act so that the ceremony is governed by common rather than statute law). As one legal historian tells us, rather archly, 'it is one of the most absurd solecisms of the twentieth century to regard concubinage as a common law marriage' (Baker, 1979, p. 395). I also avoid concubinage.

If all this seems like hard work then it should be remembered that the book is more concerned to explicate the behaviour of *the law* in picking out or rejecting certain relationships for recognition rather than how we might view them. It should be made clear at the outset that I am dealing with heterosexual relationships between one woman and one man. This is not because homosexual or 'communal' relationships are unworthy of study but because the law has not yet come near to treating the participants as other than legal strangers. An opportunity did arise in Harrogate Borough Council v. Simpson (1986 16 Fam. Law 359). In this case a woman who had lived in a lesbian relationship with the tenant of a council house claimed that she could take over the tenancy on the tenant's death. To do so, she would have had to qualify as a member of the deceased's family. Furthermore, 'family' is defined in the relevant legislation as a couple living together as husband and wife (s. 113, Housing Act 1985). The Court of Appeal rejected the claim on the basis that Parliament could not have intended a lesbian couple to be within the definition.

3. THEORETICAL CONCERNS

I am conscious that any skills I have are those of a lawyer and that interdisciplinary research is fraught with danger. By and large I rely on secondary sources and much of the literature is written within theoretical contexts that I am not competent to judge. Whilst I have tried to extract material within the context of the source itself I may not have grappled with overarching paradigms that inform the source. In dark moments, I am not sure which panel of experts I would least like to face. The methodology which I think I am bringing to bear on the material is historical materialism, in the sense that the economy is prioritised whilst allowing for relative autonomy of political, social and ideological circumstances and for those circumstances to act back on the economy. I see social class and gender as crucial mediating concepts but I avoid debates about appropriate social stratifications and the precise relationship between class and gender.

As for gender relations, I take a fairly clear-cut view that whilst a structured division of labour persists *outside* the family, it will almost inevitably exist within it. I recognise that 'the family' is also a slippery notion and discuss, in chapter 5, the extent to which it is an ideological construct partially detached from its actual representation in reality. The family generally is, of course, a major site of women's oppression but, in my view, it is marriage and its ideological, economic and legal consequences that articulates the oppressive elements. For that reason, the focus of the book is on the legal construction of marriage rather than the family.

Such strengths that there are in the book may lie in the way that I have tried to take law on board, regarding it as neither central nor wholly epiphenomenal. One of the weaknesses that I see in feminist and historical analyses of the family is an understandable reluctance to treat with legal detail, although there are, of course, exceptions. I do not see law in purely instrumental terms. In fact I am as much concerned with its ideological messages—the signals it sends out—as with the results that it might produce in any particular dispute. Indeed, one reason why it is necessary to problematise marriage and investigate its boundary is to understand when those signals arise and how they are constructed.

The word 'boundary' crops up rather a lot in the text. In chapters 2 to 4, when I deal with changes in marriage law prior to the Second World War, it signifies the point beyond which the man and woman are no longer dealt with as strangers in law. In chapters 5 and 6, marriage is largely displaced by family. This is, as I have foreshadowed, because I think that cohabitation law can only be understood within the context of a more or less articulated legal and social policy towards the family. Although 'boundary' as a legal trigger still remains the organising concept, it is in a broader setting of family and non-family. Whilst the notions of private and public are increasingly used as a paradigm, and I certainly use the terms, I am not yet sure that they really provide the basis for a complete theory. They certainly offer useful ways in to specific subjects, such as violence by men against women in the home (see, for example, Pahl, 1985). O'Donovan, on the other hand, suggests that 'it is the split between what is perceived as public (and therefore the law's business) and private (and therefore unregulated) that *accounts* for the modern legal subordination of women' (O'Donovan, 1985, p. x) (emphasis supplied). Her thesis is actually more sophisticated than this. For example, the idea that the private is unregulated is qualified so that the ideological role of the law in entering the private sphere is recognised; as is a distinction between invisible private spheres and those which are actually constituted by the public. I do not see these qualifications as contradicting the thesis itself, indeed in chapters 5 and 6 I make much the same points. Nor is it a fair criticism to say that O'Donovan is trapped within liberal philosophy (Brown, B., 1986, p. 438). The qualifications do, however, dilute the explanatory force of the thesis.

The bulk of this text was prepared prior to the publication of O'Donovan's book and some of the coverage overlaps. If references to her do not appear in all of the overlap it is because similar conclusions were arrived at independently. It should also be said that this book is more narrowly focused on the marriage trigger whereas O'Donovan deals with the larger question of sexual divisions throughout the law in a broader historical sweep. I therefore come at some of the material from a different angle and for a slightly different purpose.

2 Family and Marriage in the Mid-Eighteenth Century

1. INTRODUCTION

The combined population of England and Wales probably amounted to about 6¼ million in the mid-eighteenth century (Porter, 1982, p. 21). The two countries comprised a patchwork of local communities, each with its own traditions and heritages. Although increasingly feeling the pressure of change, it remained still a 'face-to-face' society of overwhelmingly rural character. The rural population constituted about 70 per cent of England's population (Malcolmson, 1981, p. 56). For the most part, towns were merely overgrown villages. Migration from country to town was increasing but most migrants had come less than twenty miles and many had come less than ten (Butlin, 1982, p. 28). In terms of occupation distribution, approximately 80 per cent of the population were labouring men and women and of the remaining 20 per cent probably less than 5 per cent could be called the governing class. Industry was not yet concentrated; production of textiles and the conversion of bar-iron and steel into light usable goods was still carried on, for the most part, in the homes of the workers (Briggs and Jordan, 1954, p. 182). In short, the Industrial Revolution (insofar as it is correct to call it that) had not yet happened.

In many districts there were strong ties of kinship so that much marriage was endogamous. For example, in a group of Oxfordshire villages in the second half of the century, 65 per cent of marriages involved partners who lived in the same parish (Horn, 1980, p. 14). The relative immobility of the population due to the comparatively stable rural economy is a key to our understanding of popular marriage practices. It helps account for the major role played by local normative orders, to the partial exclusion of Church and civil authorities, in the regulation of entry into marriage. Malcolmson has argued that social customs are most deeply entrenched in communities where geographical and social mobility is limited. He reasons that in a society which lacks the means of rapid transport and communications, local pecularities are likely to be highly developed, and people's sense of identity will be powerfully affected by the distinc-

9

tive traditions and circumstances of their local environment (1981, p. 93).

The notion of ritual as affirmation has caught the imagination of a number of writers. One example is Sybil Wolfram's account of kinship and marriage in England. She notes that detailed mourning customs appropriate on the death of particular relatives were not about grief but about affirming particular degrees of kinship (Wolfram, 1987, chapter 3). Another is Menefee's ethnographic study of wife-selling (to which I return later in this chapter). Menefee describes wife-selling as an informal institution and argues that 'in almost every case each institution represents an unique solution to some human condition or problem' (Menefee, 1981, p. 7). This idea is useful in the discussion of local marriage practices generally, which follows later in the chapter.

It is not only twentieth-century historians and anthropologists who recognise the importance of local custom in promoting internal solidarity. As the eighteenth century progressed and society became stratified on more modern class lines, the ruling classes became alarmed at the way that rituals were used in order to resist change. Custom provided a critical source of self-defence in a highly unequal society 'for it was one of the normative weapons of the weak against the strong, one of the ways in which power was disciplined and concessions enjoyed' (Malcolmson, 1981, p. 106). Perceptive rulers were aware that the new economic order required a more pliant and adaptable workforce that could be disciplined into the ways of wage-labour and regularity. Whilst attacks on those customs which had direct economic consequences, such as common land, poaching and smuggling, have received most attention, one should not overlook the pervasiveness of the assault. As we will see, many marriage practices were accompanied by a degree of revelry which was perceived as disruptive to efficient production and likely to pose a threat to public order. This may account for the decline in 'big weddings' as those who were socially ascendant wished to distance themselves from plebeian practices. It may also explain why complaints that Lord Hardwicke's Marriage Bill would cut right across popular procedures for marriage entry were so abruptly dismissed.

2. THE FAMILY

Whilst it may be an adequate generalisation that the eighteenth century was a critical time in the transition of the family from a unit of production to a unit of consumption, there may be a tendency in the literature on family history to jump too quickly from one to the other. At one moment we see the family as an elaborate partnership based on a small-holding with a sophisticated division of labour. At the next moment, the members of the family are reduced to factory wage-slaves under the impact of the industrial revolution (see, for example, Zaretsky, 1976, pp. 26–31). It seems more accurate to say that the separation of work and home took place at significantly different times in different trades. Some trades were more mechanised than others and even by the mid-nineteenth century many working class men and women were still working inside the home (Hall, 1982, p. 5). It is true that by about 1750 the concentration of agricultural capital had greatly increased the amount of wage-labour but a large proportion of that labour was directly involved in the productive activities of the household. Domestic labour was not readily separable from productive labour (assuming, for the moment, a clear conceptual distinction) because all family members—wives, husbands, children and elderly kin—constituted a work group (Elliot, 1986, p. 74). It was quite exceptional for there to be only one source of income for a family. Rather, the members of the family were engaged in a variety of remunerative employments, some within and some outside the home, which would vary according to the season and the market. The skilful combination of these employments, the ability to complement the talents of husband and wife and make optimum use of children and other relatives, was crucial in sustaining a regular income for the household.

Marriage remained just as much an economic partnership in the mid-eighteenth century as it was in a time when the family's property was more directly the means of production. Whilst farm labour was an important source of income, it was increasingly common for people to take up ancillary employments such as spinning, weaving, knitting, glove-making and metalwork to supplement agricultural wages, a small-holding or common rights. This is not to suggest that families were egalitarian; domestic labour and child-care were women's work and there was considerable occupational specialisation. Public power was undoubtedly male power. On the other hand, women were more easily perceived as playing a direct part in the economy than, say, a century later.

The family, then, might no longer be tied to the transmission of property through inheritance, graphically described as 'the iron chain of reproduction and inheritance' (Medick, 1976), but it remained a productive economy combining wage-labour, out-working and whatever subsistence common land could offer. It is against this background that we should view the marriage contract and appreciate that marriage practices might be uniquely related to the particular local economic substructure. Before we can look at what really happened, however, we must first sketch out the formal law.

3. MARRIAGE LAW

As far as is known, marriage formation was regarded everywhere in Europe in the first half of the middle ages as a personal and purely secular matter, almost entirely outside the law; a position which derives substantially from Roman Law. The formal history of the juridification of marriage is related by a number of writers (see, for example, Glendon, 1977, pp. 306 *et seq.* and Jackson, 1969, p. 8) but the underlying tensions and conflicts have been less comprehensively considered. The history is one of competition between three constituencies; the Church, the State and ordinary people.

In England after the Norman Conquest there followed an inexorable process of the clergy making marriage law their own province, described by one writer as 'one of the greatest seizures of social power in history' (McMurtry, 1972, p. 592). It may not be possible to provide a coherent account of ecclesiastical law because, whilst the principles appear simple, the Church courts did not apply them consistently. Furthermore, it is difficult for a lawyer unused to parallel systems of law, to understand how Church and civil law fitted together. In the late twelfth century, an ecclesiastical jurist, Peter Lombard, developed the distinction between *sponsalia per verba de praesenti* (a promise in the present tense) and *sponsalia per verba de futuro* (a promise for the future) and this distinction was accepted by Pope Alexander III. The former promise made an immediately binding marriage but the latter was bilaterally revocable prior to consummation. Once intercourse had taken place, however, the promise became complete. The Church's formally stated preference was for the marriage to be solemnised in church, preceded by triple banns (Houlbrooke, 1984, p. 78) but this was not insisted upon. The reasons for this were probably two-fold. First, the Church seems to have had a strategy of capture by stealth in the knowledge that sweeping legislation for church marriages would meet with popular opposition and avoidance. Second, and related, was the knowledge that widespread avoidance would convert into fornication what the parties believed to be marital intercourse. In other words, sins would multiply at a stroke.

After the Norman Conquest, William declared that canon law and common law should not be dispensed in the same court. This necessitated the foundation of Church courts which retained jurisdiction over laymen in matters of marriage and succession to personal property. These became known as 'the bawdy courts' because they concentrated on offences connected with sexual morality (Stone, 1977, p. 27). Much of the litigation there concerned the meaning of the promise in question (Helmholz, 1974, chapter 2 and Ingram, 1980, p. 35) and particular difficulty was occasioned by the common practice of making conditional contracts so that, for example, acceptance of the offer was made conditional on parental consent or an adequate marriage portion.

Litigation was not, however, confined to the enforcement of a promise against one party at the suit of the other. The Church itself attempted to enforce what was, in many cases, a legal fiction: that the parties had intended that the arrangement would be formally solemnised. Hence, these contracts are often confusingly referred to as precontracts, because they assumed that a further contract would be substituted. It was therefore possible for someone to be, in effect, under contract to marry someone to whom he or she was already deemed to be married. The penalties of censure and excommunication appear not to have been consistently applied. Whilst flagrant cohabitation may have been regularly punished in some areas, at some times, it is likely that failure to convert a precontract into the final contract would not attract penalty unless there was another reason why the matter was before the court. Alternatively, whilst failure to follow up a precontract at all might be punished, no action might be taken against those who subsequently did involve a priest but without complying with all the formalities.

If that seems confusing (and I have not dealt with the elaborate restrictions on marrying relatives) it is even harder to see how those rules articulated with those at common law. The common law courts had exclusive jurisdiction over all questions concerning the title to land. They were therefore concerned with the validity of marriage because it dictated two important results; the widow's right to dower and the right of the eldest legitimate son to succeed to his father's freehold land. In practice, the common law insisted that if consequences for real property were to follow then the exchange of consents had to be at least *in facie ecclesiae* (at the door of the church). This means that the common law required something more than the private exchange of promises but was satisfied with less than the Church's (theoretical) requirements. The practice may have begun by way of a direction to the jury not to believe that there had been an exchange of consents unless it had taken place in, or at the door of, a church but later was turned from a rule of evidence into a substantive rule of law.

It is important to be clear that any other marriages might be *valid* as far as the common law was concerned. They were simply ineffective for real property and related purposes. What were becoming known as irregular marriages meant that subsequent marriage ceremonies might be void for bigamy; see, for example, Wigmore's Case ([1706] 2 Salk 437). When I trace the origins of Lord Hardwicke's Act in the next chapter I will spell out further the problems that this caused for the orderly transmission of property and look at some earlier attempts at statutory control over clandestine marriages. For the purposes of understanding the marriage practices of most ordinary people, however, this outline should suffice for the present chapter.

4. MARRIAGE IN PRACTICE

I said earlier that the history of marriage is one of competition between three constituencies—the Church, the State and ordinary people. In this section I concentrate on the third constituency. Insofar as most people ever concerned themselves with the right of the Church to dictate methods by which they should marry, or bothered to justify their departure from the Church's prescriptions, their attitude was probably one of resentment at interference in the hallowed customs of their neighbourhood. Had they been in a position to read sixteenth-century French satirists, they might well have agreed with Rabelais in condemning that 'tyrannical presumption' which led priests and monks, unmarried themselves, to 'meddle with, obtrude upon, and thrust their sickles into, harvests of secular business' (Lasch, 1974, p. 90).

Quaife's investigation into sexual relations amongst the non-gentry in seventeenth-century Somerset may throw light on what we know about informal marriage in the mid-eighteenth century. His thesis, briefly, is that 'the decision as to which sexual acts remained illicit and the punishment of those engaged in such acts rested with three sometimes overlapping, but generally exclusive jurisdictions—the Church, the State and custom enforced by the local community' (Quaife, 1979, p. 194). By and large people were amoral, in the sense that they judged others' actions by the social and economic consequences rather than by moral precept. Adultery and prostitution were likely to lead to a breach of the peace, pre-marital intercourse (if it could not be converted into marriage itself) was likely to lead to the mother and child being a charge on the parish. If the conduct was to be judged at all, it was more in these terms than on the grounds of sinfulness.

In 1700 throughout Europe as a whole only 50 per cent of women married and marriage was frequently the goal for economic survival. In some cases, marriage was literally a matter of life and death. Branca suggests that in the countryside, women of twenty who never married could expect to live nine years less than their married sisters (1978, p. 73). Whilst the proportion of women never marrying was always lower in England anyway, by mid-century the proportion never marrying fell to 7 per cent (Alderman, 1986, p. 2). The mean age at marriage also dropped. In the course of the eighteenth century the mean age of men marrying fell from 27.5 to 26.2, and for women from 26.4 to 24.9 (Gillis, 1985, p. 110). Undoubtedly the underlying reason lies in the changing economic structure. As a general rule, expanding economic opportunities increase the nuptiality rate and decrease the age of first marriage. But the effect of the economy on nuptiality operated regionally and its effects were mediated by local occupational structures. In some areas, the practice of servants 'living in' declined so that there were fewer restraints on courtship. Before 1834, poor relief policy discriminated against single people so that the choice was sometimes between migrating and marrying. Where realistic migration possibilities were low, the attraction of marriage increased. When I look at community control over marriage entry and the steps that the young took to evade that control we will see how family formation articulated with prevailing economic conditions.

Outhwaite has observed that a social history of marriage 'is a near impossible task, and no one book can do justice to the complexities of special variety and historical change' (Outhwaite, 1980, p. 1). One masterful attempt is that of Gillis (1985) and because I am not convinced that he fully embraces 'alternative' practices it is as well to outline his arguments here before turning to those practices. Gillis draws a basic distinction between betrothal or little weddings and big weddings. The former constituted the precontract for legal purposes (with the effect that a marriage came into being, particularly if intercourse took place) whilst the latter would normally satisfy the full requirements of Church and common law. Betrothal was a distinct phase, a liminal situation, between being single and being fully married. Psychologically it enabled each party to move out of the homosocial world, that is, of socialising only with others of the same gender, into the heterosocial world of marriage with the expectations that it carried. Betrothal marked a period of seclusion for the couple so that they could think things through and gather resources together. It was also a period of making sure that the match was suitable in all senses.

The big wedding was accompanied by elaborate ritual and festivities. These could be a threat to social order. Weddings could produce great hostilities and envy; be it from disappointed suitors, friends who felt shunned and elders who disapproved of setting up any new family in the community or of that particular one. Some of the rough peri-nuptial practices, involving effigies, curses and acts of direct violence seem designed to dissipate tensions within the community.

Gillis's account of the distinctions between little and big weddings seems to fit well with the legal distinctions between precontracts, or spousals, on the one hand and formal marriage on the other, particularly for the period until about 1750. By then, he says, the system was fragmenting. It was particularly suited to an economy based on small-holdings but as society became more sharply stratified those at the upper end became increasingly snooty about common practices and preferred more privacy in their weddings. Even amongst the lower orders there was a desire to evade the community controls over family formation as greater access to wage labour made the young more self-sufficient. Women had enjoyed considerable freedoms within the period of courtship and as the elder generation sought to increase the regulation of marriage, perhaps in an attempt to restore some certainty in a changing world, and prevent resources being drained when small-holdings were under threat, women pressed for their right to elect their future spouses. Anti-clericalism was fuelled by the fees that the clergy charged for weddings. Strengthening non-conformism introduced a plurality of notions about the meaning of marriage. The movement was therefore towards clandestinity in solemnising the marriage or even against solemnising at all so that the earlier informal stage became also the final stage. Gillis does also pay attention to the ways in which betrothals did *not* fit in with legal precontracts. Betrothals, he says, 'placed the man under obligations to support or marry (*sic*) the woman should pregnancy result. On the other hand, his liability in terms of property was strictly limited. In the Lake District a handfast [discussed below] was supposed to last no longer than a year and a day. If at that time either party wished to end the relationship, they had a customary right to do so. Similar time limits were in effect in Wales and on the Isle of Portland' (Gillis, 1985, p. 50). Betrothals and the clandestine informal marriages that gradually succeeded them were clearly regarded as conditional, intermediate statuses that could be terminated by the consent of the parties, whereas this was not the legal position; certainly once intercourse had taken place. At the risk of sounding impudent by challenging a scholar on his own specialism and in his own discipline, my reservation is that deviations from strict Church and State rules are seen first as elaborations upon them rather than expressions of views *alternative* to the orthodox position. The result is that later practices in the period with which we are specifically concerned are seen as mutations of those elaborations rather than wholly new forms thrown up by new circumstances. To amplify this reservation I turn first to a discussion of the practices themselves and then to a functional analysis.

Estimates of the extent of informal marriage in the first half of the eighteenth century vary. Some historians have settled for a figure of one-fifth whilst others have put it as high as one half (Stone, 1979, p. 31). Because informal marriage tended to be peculiar to certain areas, it is probable that any average figure would mask the fact that in some regions these customs were prevalent whilst in others they were less so and marriage in church was more common. Furthermore there is a lack of clarity as to what is being talked about. Whilst a marriage in church after the due publication of banns and perform- ance of other conditions was clearly the most formal, it seems that clergymen still had a role in many marriages outside the church. The priest's traditional function as a mediator of disputes in the commun- ity (Baker, 1973, p. 131) meant that he might side with a young couple seeking to marry against their parents' wishes and act as a notary (Houlbrooke, 1979, pp. 57–66). Our main concern here, however, is not with those marriage forms which occupy the space between irregular and regular marriage but with those which might not have counted as marriage at all under ecclesiastical or civil law.

Probably the best-known secular marriage custom is the broomstick wedding, or besom marriage: (a besom is a type of brush made
out of twigs, usually from a birch tree). The Welsh folklorist who
wrote under the name Gwenith Gwyn interviewed a seventy-three
year old woman in the 1920s who described the process as follows
(Gwyn, 1928, pp. 153–4):

> A birch besom was placed aslant in the open doorway of a house,
> with the head of the besom on the doorstone, and the top of the
> handle on the doorpost. Then the young man jumped over it first
> into the house, and afterwards the young woman in the same way.
> The jumping was not recognised as marriage if either of the two
> touched the besom in jumping or, by accident, removed it from its
> place. It was necessary to jump in the presence of witnesses too.

The expression 'jumping the broom' is still used in parts of Wales
today, particularly in the north, to describe an irregular union, as is
the term broomstick wedding (Jones, 1930, p. 185). Similar
metaphors are used in parts of England. Robert Roberts' account of
working class life in Salford at the turn of the century refers to the
lack of criticism of those living 'over't brush' despite the otherwise
strict moral code concerning sexual matters in the community
(Roberts, 1971, p. 47).

'Leaping the broomstick' was not confined to England and Wales.
Baker says that gypsy couples across Europe married in this way. The
broom was decorated with sweet-scented yellow flowers to benefit the
couple's fertility. 'If the woman's skirt touches the branch it shows
that she has lost her virginity or is pregnant on the wedding day; if the
man's trousers touch the broom he will prove unfaithful. Both leap
high' (Baker, 1977, pp. 50–1). One still hears of marriages today
where the bride shakes the hand of a chimney-sweep after the
ceremony. This presumably derives from the ancient symbolisms
attached to the brush in pagan times.

Another form of ceremony was handfasting, which literally means
'pledging the hand' (Fielding, 1961, p. 290). It was prevalent in
remoter areas, particularly in the Scottish Highlands and border
country, Wales and the extreme south-west. It involved the exchange
of promises before witnesses with the man and woman joining hands.
The couple lived together for a year and a day and, if pleased with the
arrangement, could extend it for life (Baker, 1977, p. 32). The
conception of a child within the time limit made the union binding
and the child, in Scotland at any rate, enjoyed full succession rights.

Gillis's discussion of besom marriage relates to the period after Lord Hardwicke's Marriage Act 1753, when it was clearly an alternative practice. He does not refer to it in an earlier period (when it undoubtedly existed) and this may be, as I have said, because he relegates the existence of marriage systems wholly alternative to that of betrothal followed by big wedding or precontract followed by full contract. I develop this argument by taking a functional analysis of popular customs; in other words by suggesting how they might fit with a local scheme of things which had little reference to the prescriptions of Church or State.

(a) Community Control

A recurrent problem for most communities was to ensure a male provider for women and children. One response was what we might call processual marriage; in other words where the formation of marriage was regarded as a *process* rather than a clearly defined rite of passage. Recent evidence suggests that in many cases consent to intercourse and consent to marriage were not separated analytically and were perhaps deliberately blurred in some communities. In Quaife's study of sexual behaviour in Somerset we note that (Quaife, 1979, p. 61):

> In effect for the peasant community there was very little premarital sex. Most of the acts seen as such by Church and State were interpreted by the village as activities within marriage—a marriage begun with the promise and irreversibly confirmed by pregnancy.

This promise was often presumed by local opinion so as to avoid illegitimacy and any consequent charge on the rates. The man was a husband and obliged to maintain his wife and children. It was not only the community which gained control this way. The knowledge that a marriage would be locally implied from the fact of pregnancy gave power to women who were concerned that the man might desert them. The approach to sex was therefore far from casual: it was located in a general belief in the ability of public opinion to command obedience to community values (Golby and Purdue, 1984, p. 47; Alderman, 1986, p. 3).

Anthea Newman's study of the east Kent parish of Ash-Next-Sandwich illustrates the broad view of what constituted marriage. She found that 'the priest's attitude to stable unions was unpredictable' and cites a case where one family had six bastards (*sic*) but four of them were registered as legitimate (Newman, 1980, p. 146). E.A. Wrigley's work on the parish registers of Tetbury in Gloucestershire for the 1690s supports this. He discovered that there was a separate category of marriage entry where the groom's name alone was entered and no date was mentioned. This would suggest that certain priests were doing their best to register what the *community* regarded as marriages even though the relevant statute (in this case the Marriage Act 1695) made no provision for such entries (Wrigley, 1973, p. 15). As we will see in chapter 4, some clergy were prepared to notarise these arrangements even after the 1753 Act, when there was no conceivable legal validity and when the priest was liable to fourteen years' transportation. This must support the view that they were prepared to do so in the first half of the century.

   This flexible (and perhaps retroactive) form of marriage performed an important function within the community by enabling social mores and pressure to create a marriage (and thus support obligations) without the need to force the couple into a church. It was strengthened by the clergy's willingness, in some cases, to notarise the marriage retrospectively. Much community control operated to *discourage* marriage where there was no pregnancy, rather than create it when there was, and this is illustrated by the function of informal marriage in evading that control.

(b)   Evading Control

Frequent reference to community may create the impression of idyllic societies characterised by consensus over basic issues and sweetened by quaint ritual. In fact, at a personal level, communities were sometimes racked by conflict. Many accounts of informal marriage practices reveal a desire by the participants to be hidden from the public gaze in the knowledge that their actions would ultimately receive public sanction. The main reason why formal marriage offended many couples' desire for privacy was the requirement that banns announcing the forthcoming marriage had to be read in the local church. Canon law had stipulated since at least 1604 that a church wedding must take place between the hours of 8.00 a.m. and noon in the church at the place of residence of one of the pair after the banns had been read for three consecutive weeks. Allied to this requirement was the provision that marriages of persons under twenty-one were forbidden without the consent of parents or guardians. The necessity of banns was formally to enable anyone to object, for example because of lack of parental consent, a previous marriage or consanguinity (closeness of blood). It operated to mobilise general opposition to the marriage which might be hard to resist. Parents could make real the threat of withholding a portion for the daughter. Peers and elders could mount psychological and material pressure to dissuade the couple. Even if one of the couple was under twenty-one and there was no parental consent, the banns were still necessary because, although the marriage was forbidden and the clergyman liable to penalties, it was still binding for life: a paradox, says Stone, which 'the laity found hard to understand' (1979, p. 31). One way round marriage by banns was to obtain a licence. During the sixteenth and seventeenth centuries the sale of licences increased but their availability was patchy, depending on the attitude of the bishop and their cost.

Young people wishing to present the world with a *fait accompli* might be able to enlist the support of a sympathetic clergyman who would act as a witness to a private agreement. Many clergymen lacked a benefice and preferred to risk sanctions rather than lose income (Wynne, 1955, p. 8) but if there was no such assistance then others were prepared to help. There are many accounts of local lay people setting up in direct competition with the Church. Gillis refers to laymen like the Bristol barber, John Boroston, and the Berkshire dairyman, Gabriell Rose, who used public houses as their place of solemnisation (Gillis, 1980, p. 5). Whilst the local pub might seem a conspicuous spot to choose for a couple wishing to keep their union secret, there is a distinction between keeping their *plans* secret (which banns made difficult) and concealing the event itself. Market forces were at work in Llanyckil in Wales where the local clergyman found himself in competition with Evan Cadwalader, a blacksmith, who ran his marriage business from nearby Bala. Cadwalader in turn was competing with the Reverend James Langford who was prepared to defy the canon law and ignore both banns and licence—for a fee.

Many adults too might have wished to maintain secrecy about their wedding: widows or widowers marrying 'too soon' after the death of a spouse or against the wishes of their family; couples disparate in age, social status or religion; bigamists and bankrupts all had reason to seek privacy (Outhwaite, 1973, p. 64). But there was a specific reason why the young turned to informal marriage at about this time and that is the increase in inter-generational conflict. Such conflict should be understood as having an economic basis connected with the available resources of the area; in particular the dominant form of property and wealth. In a time when wealth was related to land-holding (and productive land in England and Wales was a limited resource) a strategy of late marriage was a means of regulating population growth generally, and the age composition of the population in particular.

Jarrett makes this point rather neatly when he says that 'for the great majority of people in eighteenth century England, the most urgent problem in life was how to prevent it' (1976, p. 58). It is true that various methods of contraception were used. *Coitus interruptus* was widely practised and contraceptive sheaths were available, at least in the towns. Abortion and infanticide were other methods of population control. But the most effective method was, of course, abstinence and a correlation can be made between areas of late marriage and scarcity of resources. Jarrett may not be entirely accurate in saying that the major desire was to avoid children altogether: rather, it was to strike the right balance. In Porter's words, 'too few able bodies and the depleted workforce would not sustain well-being. Too many mouths and pauperism would edge in' (1982, p. 161).

A local policy of late marriage had to be enforced and the withholding of parental consent or approval was only one such method. Courting practices and degradation ceremonies are now understood as elements of a more comprehensive programme to safeguard the local economy by discouraging early or unwise marriages and exogamous marriage (that is with those from outside the area). As Levine says, 'the people of the village community enforced the strategies of family formation they had themselves created to promote a form of stability, an optimisation of the demo-economic balance so far as the group was concerned' (1977, p. 148). Why should the eighteenth century see an exacerbation of intergenerational conflict? The answer appears to lie in the gradual breakup of traditional family patterns due to the increase in wage labour (Medick, 1976, p. 303). The foundation and continuing existence of the family as a unit of production and consumption was decreasingly dependent on the transmission of property through inheritance. There were now real possibilities of founding a family primarily on wage labour. This loosened the structural connection of the generations by releasing the young from the patriarchal domination that reliance on inheritance allowed. But the towns and cities of the mid century did not yet have abundant factory employment to enable the young to emigrate. Instead their wages came from the land and social practices were still locked in the force of tradition. One speculates that this contradiction between the opportunities of the new and the restraints of the old greatly heightened the inevitable strains existing between adolescence and adulthood. Informal marriage, particularly if it took place before a credible witness, evaded the local crises that would result if a campaign was allowed to mount so that parents and the community at large simply had to make the best of it. The union might or might not then be followed by a formal marriage, now that the couple could not be unmarried.

Another group wishing to evade control who would not go on to a church marriage were nonconformists wishing to escape from Anglican control. It is probable that in many regions there was a latent dislike of the idea of church marriage. When we consider the effects of the Civil Marriage Act 1836, we will see that in certain areas the use of the register office was startlingly high (something like 65 per cent of all marriages) and one suggestion is that these areas had had a tradition of non-church marriage which the new procedure drew upon. One fascinating insight is Christopher Hill's study of radical thinking and beliefs in the Interregnum (Hill, 1975). During the period 1645–53 the English cultural world was turned upside down. The grip of the Church was loosened and censorship laws were relaxed or unenforced. Fermented by the unsettled political climate and breakdown of structures of established authority, radical ideas flourished concerning a wide range of political, economic and social matters. One such matter was marriage. Pamphlets were published denouncing the growth industry of expensive marriage licenses, which, as Hill says, must have predisposed the poor to despise church marriage. Whilst I am dealing with a later period, one can speculate that in a country comprising self-contained and relatively closed communities, similar distrust of the Church's marriage industry may have continued, albeit underground due to re-imposed censorship.

One particular cultural factor relating to Wales was that of language. A large proportion of the inhabitants in the eighteenth century were Welsh monoglots (Pryce, 1978–80, p. 26). If the local bishop decided that marriages should be conducted in English then they would be incomprehensible to many participants. It seems that one bishop did not even know which language his clergy used because in 1749 the Bishop of Bangor instituted an enquiry. For Welsh monoglots, dissenters and catholics, the simple exchange of consents before a credible witness was sufficient and, if it mattered, had some recognition in civil law.

(c) Equal Rights

The formal legal position was that on marriage the ownership of a woman's personal property passed to her husband along with control of her real property. Her legal capacity was, in effect, suspended whilst she was under her husband's 'couverture'. As I will demonstrate in the next chapter, the propertied classes made use of marriage settlements to evade the harsher consequences of these rules but, whilst not wanting to romanticise the past, there is evidence that humbler folk developed informal marriage for a similar purpose. The belief was that certain procedures allowed the woman to retain separate legal identity and property. This was more pronounced in a later period as practices suited to urbanisation were thrown up, but there are examples of popular forms in the mid-eighteenth century. One is the besom wedding where, according to some of Gwenith Gwyn's informants, jumping the broom enabled brides to retain their maiden names, their property and their rights to the children (Gwyn, 1928, p. 156). Another is the smock wedding which achieved the same end. The belief was that if a woman was married wearing only her smock, her financial obligations and assets remained entirely separate from those of her husband. An extract from the parish register of Masham in Yorkshire describes such a wedding in June 1723:

> The woman, to prevent a creditor coming on her newly-wedded husband for debts contracted by her former husband, had nothing to cover her nakedness during the solemnising of the wedding but her shift.

The thinking behind this procedure appears to have been that if she brought neither clothes nor property with her, then her creditors were hamstrung. It is not known how effective smock weddings were in the face of a creditor, or a husband, who preferred resort to canon and common law to local normative orders. More effective protection for women may have been local provision for retrospective marriage, which I have already discussed, and trial marriage and *de facto* divorce which I discuss under the gender-neutral heading of incompatibility.

(d) Incompatibility

Macfarlane (1986, p. 306) doubts the existence of trial marriage, at least insofar as it might be a test of fertility, and argues that whilst sexual compatibility was important, fecundity was not. His general thesis is that England was unique in marrying within its resources. Following his earlier work on the origins of English individualism (Macfarlane, 1978) he suggests that the ubiquity of wage labour meant that it was often economically unwise to have children. Whereas in most other societies a familial mode of production based on the land implied that marriage, procreation and wealth were seen to go together, the individualism produced by wage labour made marriage a union of individuals rather than a match between families and landholdings. Whilst Macfarlane presents a compelling case in support of a Malthusian view of population control, his work is pitched at a high level of generality which has the strengths of an anthropological history but is weak in terms of regional and class specificity. The picture I am trying to sketch is one of great regional disparity in marriage forms with a high degree of congruence between those forms and the prevailing economic substructure. There is a large amount of evidence to support the existence of fertility testing, much of which is not cited by Macfarlane, the work of J.R. Gillis (1985) being the obvious example.

In some rural communities the production of children was an economic necessity, because children could be productive at an early age, whereas in others children would simply drain scarce resources. With the advent of industrialisation and the increase in out-working, children were useful in assisting cottage workers and, of course, when factory production gradually took over from cottage industry, the children's wage earnings were an important supplement to the family income. In the longer term, the prospect of having a number of children surviving to adulthood was an important insurance for the parents when they grew old.

The couple would also have to be compatible in a non-biological sense. As I mentioned earlier, family incomes in the eighteenth century generally came from a number of sources and a successful combination of the spouses' skills was central to economic survival. The logical consequence of the need to ensure fertility and compatibility was some form of trial marriage. We have already looked at the notion of processual marriage in the context of marriages being created retrospectively to ensure the support of dependent women and children. We can also see it from another angle by regarding it as a deliberate and conscious device to ensure compatibility.

In chapter 1, I used the early work of the Cambridge Group for the History of Population and Social Structure as an illustration of a rather simple view of marriage. Their re-evaluation of illegitimacy statistics is based on a recognition that parents may have been informally married with a view to having children and that a subsequent full ceremony may not have been regarded as necessary. Baker has described handfasting in this light (1977, p. 23) as has Fielding with regard to Scotland (1961, p. 292). Wales in particular had a tradition of dissolubility of marriage within a fixed period in order to confirm fertility. In medieval times the marriage was not indissoluble until seven years had passed. Giraldus Cambrensis, a Welsh medieval churchman, asserted that the Welsh 'are not accustomed to undertake the responsibility of marriage without proof of compatibility, and, above all, of fertility, through cohabitation and intercourse' (Williams, 1908, p. 195).

The Island of Portland probably provides the clearest examples of trial marriage. There are numerous accounts of the practice there (see, for example, Fielding, 1961, p. 75 and Horn, 1980). If no pregnancy occurred then the couple might break off relations but whilst the trial continued there were strict duties of fidelity. Gillis (1985, p. 126) describes Portland as a clannish place where marriage never took place until the woman is pregnant. Local enforcement was so strong (reluctant males would be stoned out of the island) that there was virtually no illegitimacy there. Thomas Hardy's nineteenth-century fantasy *The Well-Beloved* is set on the fictional island of Slingers, which is meant to represent Portland. The plot centres on the conflict between the 'new education' of Victorian morality and the tradition of pre-marital pregnancy.

Portland fits in well with Gillis's scheme of betrothal followed by full marriage because the pregnancy was meant to occasion marriage rather than constitute it but, as we have seen, there were areas where pregnancy and marriage were not analytically separated. In those parts where betrothal was a common preliminary we also see elements of trial. These varied from night-visiting and bundling where the suitor might, without disgrace, spend the night with his intended one (practices differed over the extent to which intercourse was intended to take place or at least overlooked) to cohabitation being permissible during the betrothal. With the latter, separation prior to pregnancy need cause no loss of honour for either party.

Trial marriage therefore embraced the possibility of *de facto* divorce (it would not be a trial without it). Even where the trial period was over there were occasions when informal divorce was possible. A fully social account of divorce and its history waits to be written. Brief reference to it here, however, strengthens my argument about the existence of informal legal systems which ran parallel to formal ones. More or less permanent desertion was regarded in some areas as morally dissolving a marriage (Stone, 1979, p. 35). Wife-selling was a ritualised version of informal divorce. Thomas Hardy's *The Mayor of Casterbridge* begins with a wife-sale and in defending himself against an outraged Victorian public Hardy assured them that the practice was well-known in rural areas and not a figment of his imagination (Mueller, 1957, p. 567). Menefee (1981) suggests that many, if not most, wife-sales took place with the wife's consent, or at least acquiescence. It was common, however, for the wife to be led to a public mock auction with a halter around her neck and this hardly promotes cool reflection.

Jumping the broom can be regarded both as trial marriage and informal divorce. In Wales it was possible for the couple to jump backwards over the broom in the presence of witnesses (Gwyn, 1928, p. 156). As the basis of the marriage was purely that of consent, without the intervention of the Church, then mutual consent was considered equally effective to revoke the contract. Menefee (1981, p. 20) quotes one nineteenth-century song which presumably draws on older traditions:

> So let us be married my Mary,
> If ever dislike be our lot,
> We jump'd o'er the broom, then an airy
> jump back shall unfasten the knot.

5. CONCLUSION

Prior to Lord Hardwicke's Act 1753 there was a plurality of marriage forms. Where the formal prescriptions of canon and common law did not suit local requirements, alternative practices were developed which did. Many of these had some reference to the general law so that, for example, the betrothal stage operated as the exchange of consents. But even here the possibility of discharging the agreement in the event of incompatibility often departed from the principle that the precontract was indissoluble. Other practices are best seen as wholly alternative to the general law, so that any connection one makes with it is an *ex post facto* rationalisation. As Goody (1983, p. 183) says of alternative normative orders, they 'cannot simply be regarded as variants on a common, written theme, for they may represent different interests, different ideologies, and may thus stand in marked opposition to the other mode'.

In the remainder of the book I hope to develop the idea that private ordering of family relationships co-exists with public ordering by looking at the processes by which the public boundary is constructed and at the popular reactions to the boundary. I am seeking to demonstrate that a continuity can be traced between pre-1754 practices and more recent ones. That continuity is not so much a linear causal phenomenon, so I am not suggesting, for example, that today's cohabitees are in any way conscious successors of earlier informal spouses. The continuity is more a common tendency of men and women to negotiate with legal, economic and social realities and, within limits, to carve out a living arrangement which makes greater sense than the State sanctioned form.

3 Lord Hardwicke's Act 1753: The Landed Embrace the Loaded

1. INTRODUCTION

On 25 March 1754 The Marriage Act 1753 came into force. It was entitled 'An Act for the better preventing of clandestine marriages'. Briefly, its provisions were as follows. All marriages in any place other than in a church or public chapel, and without banns or licence, were to be 'null and void to all Intents and Purposes whatsoever'. Detailed rules were laid down concerning the publication of banns in the parish of the parties upon 'three Sundays preceding the Solemnization of Marriage during the Time of Morning Service, or Evening Service (if there be no Morning Service in such Church or Chapel upon any of the Sundays)'. The parson could refuse to publish the first banns unless he had been given at least seven days notice of the parties' names and place of residence. If a parent declared dissent to the proposed marriage at the time when the banns were published then that publication was void.

The issue of licenses, which avoided the need for banns, was also closely regulated. At least one of the parties must have resided in the area of the relevant church for the previous four weeks before the licence could be issued. In effect, therefore, the residence requirement was substantially the same for marriage by banns or licence because one should add seven days notice to the parson to the three weeks of banns. All marriages solemnised by licence where either of the parties (not being a widow or widower) was under the age of twenty-one were also 'absolutely null and void to all Intents and Purposes whatsoever' without the consent of the father of the minor. Curiously, a marriage by banns without the requisite paternal consent was not vitiated and this may have been a drafting error. If it was intended, the reason may have been that banns gave greater publicity, and therefore warning to the parents, than the issue of a licence (Blackstone, 1857, vol. I, p. 455).

An elaborate system was set out to enforce the basic provisions of the Act. Any person wilfully and knowingly solemnising a marriage

29

in any place other than a church or public chapel without the requisite banns or licence was to be transported to America for fourteen years. Detailed rules were made for the maintenance of registers of all marriages and banns, even down to the type of paper and the method of pagination. The marriage itself had to be in the presence of two or more credible witnesses, apart from the celebrating minister. The parties and the minister had then to sign the entry in the register stating whether the marriage was by banns or licence. If a marriage by licence involved a minor, the entry had to state that paternal consent had been given. The signatures were then attested by the witnesses. Any person intentionally taking part in any irregularities concerning the register, the publication of banns or the issue of a licence 'shall be guilty of a Felony, and shall suffer Death as a Felon, without Benefit of Clergy'. To ensure publicity of the Act, it had to be read in all parish churches on specified occasions in the first two years of its operation.

Lord Hardwicke's Act did not apply to the Royal Family, to the marriages of Quakers or Jews or to marriages outside England and Wales. With those exceptions, however, it was a comprehensive strategy of policing the young and preventing bigamy. The provisions were harsh and inelastic. The Act swept away any legal validity that precontracts and other informal marriages might have had. To make this clear, it was provided that no case could be brought in an ecclesiastical court to compel a marriage *in facie ecclesiae* by virtue of an earlier contract. A modern lawyer might now say that there could be no order for specific performance of the contract, although there might be an action for damages at common law for breach of promise (which was not abolished until 1970).

In this chapter I try to produce an account of the passage of the Act which goes beyond its immediate and precipitate causes and deals with underlying structural reasons why the Act was felt necessary. I also try to explain why the Act took the form it did. Briefly, my argument is that two profound economic changes were under way at this time; the further re-organisation of agriculture along capitalist lines and the emergence of a strong merchant and trade sector. This affected the nature of marriage amongst the propertied classes in contradictory ways. The centrality of primogeniture was to a certain extent undermined because increasingly the marriages of all children, not just the eldest surviving son, became important occasions for capital accumulation. On the other hand, capitalist social relations brought with them an intensification of pressure for companionate marriage based on romantic love. So at the very time when patriarchy wanted greater control over the marriage of children, the children wanted to be free of that pressure. The legislation, although only pertinent to the propertied classes, was applied to virtually all the population because it was enacted against the background of hegemonic strategies to disseminate a new world view. I will qualify some of these assertions later but, in outline, the analysis rests on the axes of class, gender and generation. The victor was propertied patriarchy.

2. STRUCTURAL CHANGES IN ECONOMY AND MARRIAGE

Until the eighteenth century, the means of production (in the sense of property which could produce wealth) was overwhelmingly land. England, more than any other European country, had a long tradition of alienability of land (Macfarlane, 1978, chapter 4) but marriage and death were still the most significant events upon which freehold land changed hands. Primogeniture was a rule of law whereby the eldest male in the same degree succeeded to his ancestor's land there being contingency rules in the event of there being only a more remote male. It operated on death in default of any other arrangement. Normally a lifetime arrangement would be made through an entail or settlement but this usually preserved the principle of primogeniture whilst making provision for other relatives and various contingencies. An entail was a legal document which settled the succession of an estate inalienably upon descendants in a specifically described order of preference. The effectiveness of the entail varied over time but by 1650 lawyers had developed a new device, the strict settlement. This vested the property in trustees and appointed the heir as a tenant for life. At this stage in legal history the tenant for life had no power to sell the property and so the property could be tied to the family. If the settlement was made on the occasion of a marriage then the patrimony would be preserved for the eldest son of the marriage, or failing a son, for the next or closest male relative. Provision was made for the bride in the event of her being widowed and for any daughters or younger sons (Stone and Stone, 1984, p. 73). Despite the name, settlements were not particularly strict, partly because of rules against perpetuities which limited the number of future generations to which the land could be tied, and partly because there had to be some flexibility in the system and so the documents were not drafted to apply too far ahead. Land often had to be sold off or partitioned; for example to meet a crisis or provide marriage portions for daughters. Consequently, every so often a new settlement would be required and one major occasion for making it would be the marriage of the eldest son.

As a result of the regular need to remodel the settlement parents had to have effective control over the marriage although that control might rarely be exercised. One such method would be notice of any unwise match by the eldest son so that heavy persuasion could be brought to bear if he was over 21 and an objection to the banns or licence could be made if he was a minor. Equally important was sufficient notice of a wise match so that the appropriate documents could be drafted and, perhaps, negotiations carried out within the wider family. But it was not only the eldest son who needed to be controlled. Changes were afoot which meant that younger children were not simply reserves in the event of the heir dying prematurely. First, there was an acceleration in the circulation of agricultural land. This may not have been so amongst the county elite; the relatively small number of landowners, probably titled, who had enormous wealth and national political influence, with which the Stones are concerned (Stone and Stone, 1984). It was more so with the lower level of gentry.

More advanced methods of farming led to the concentration of agricultural land in fewer hands as the more efficient bought out the less so. Legal devices emerged which allowed some entails to be barred so that the land could be sold, thus increasing the stock of unencumbered land in circulation. Enclosure Acts brought more scientific farming methods to large tracts of land. The conversion of leases for lives into leases for a fixed term of years gave more commercial certainty to freeholders. Speculation abroad increased and this led to spectacular failures (for example the South Sea Bubble in 1720) as well as successes. Land had to be sold off to pay debts. Increasingly hedonistic life-styles amongst the gentry led to over-spending and polite retirement to spa towns, typified by Sir Walter Elliot's removal to Bath in Jane Austen's *Persuasion*.

At the same time we see the growth of merchant and industrial capital; in other words, wealth not directly linked to land. Economic activity had been rising steadily during the reigns of the Stuarts in the seventeenth century but the development of the colonies and free-dom from major wars during the early eighteenth century provided considerable boosts. Feinstein estimates that in 1760, durable assets other than land already amounted to slightly less than a third of the national capital of Great Britain and the proportion was growing rapidly. By 1850 it amounted to over one half (Feinstein, 1981, p. 128). Chesterman (1984) demonstrates that over the period 1750–1914 the subject matter of the trust changed from overwhelmingly land to personal property; for example government stocks and loans on mortgage. Government stocks were a major competitor with land for capital as early as 1747 (Stone and Stone, 1984, p. 13).

These developments had profound effects on marriage practices of the wealthy. Marriage now became a crucial alliance in a new sense; an alliance of different types of capital. Agricultural wealth provided stability and steady income; commercial wealth was higher-risk growth capital. Together they formed a balanced portfolio with the latter helping to finance improvements in the former. There was also a more intimate connection between the two. Land was the best security in the growing practice of raising money on mortgage in order to invest it in trade. What better occasion for the two to come together than a marriage between the children of each sector? Porter puts this neatly when he says that the 'alliance of a gentleman's son with a merchant's daughter, the landed embracing the loaded, was marriage à la mode' (Porter, 1982, p. 66).

The new marriage as an inter-class bargain was widely perceived at the time. Hogarth's set of prints *Marriage à la Mode*, to which Porter alludes, concerned the marriage of a rakish landed heir to the heiress of a city merchant. Sir William Temple, writing in the late seventeenth century moaned (Lecky, 1883, vol. i, p. 193):

> I think I remember within less than fifty years, the first noble families that married into the city for downright money and thereby introduced by degrees this public grievance which has since ruined so many estates by the necessity of giving good portions to daughters.

The last part of this quotation provides the key to the argument of this chapter. The new marriage differed from the old because *all* children were now strategically useful. Younger sons could attract merchants' daughters and vice versa. Merchants' daughters were valuable because primogeniture was less applicable to the new form of wealth. In any event, the emergent bourgeoisie, who held certain ideologies about fairness, were more likely to treat their children equally and distribute wealth amongst them (Harrison and Mort,

1980, p. 85). The Stones, whilst acknowledging the 'economic and cultural symbiosis of land and money', suggest that, despite contemporary accounts that these marriages were common, there was a widely held view that it was not permissible for a landed family to marry its daughter to a tradesman or his heir. On the other hand, it was permissible to trade status for money and marry one's son to the heiress of a tradesman (Stone and Stone, 1984, pp. 247–251). As I have said, the Stones concentrate on the upper elite and it may be that the popular perception was correct for the tiers below (Clark, 1985, p. 71). In any event, even if the landed classes were relatively endogamous in practice, the perception itself would be enough to heighten parents' concern over policing their children's marriages.

But what of these children? The fiction reading young were becoming intoxicated with the idea of marriage based on romantic love and personal compatibility. The origin of affective marriage is a subject of much debate amongst social historians. There are marxist versions (Weeks, 1981, chapter 2), idealist versions (Stone, 1979), attempts to steer a path between the two (Shorter, 1977) and confronting all these is Macfarlane (1978 and 1986). Attempts to show that the provisions in strict settlements in this period support the theory of affective marriage have been convincingly attacked (Spring, 1984). Whatever the origins, however, the conditions by the mid-eighteenth century certainly enabled romantic attachments to flourish. Porter says that a 'season of Balls, family parties and visits to resorts such as Bath had to be invented to give Miss more chance to sound eligible suitors' (Porter, 1982, p. 43). By the end of the seventeenth century many of the elite spent six months of the year away from their country seat (Stone and Stone, 1984, p. 37):

> This development, and the social contacts outside the county that it bred, fostered the growth of a national marriage market. London became a central matrimonial clearing house, with scriveners, attorneys, solicitors and clergy acting as sources of information on likely prospects, while balls, parties and assemblies served as supervised meeting places for the young.

The fiction of the time increasingly dealt with the conflict between marrying for love and marrying for money. It abounded with references to secret weddings. This leads us away from structural causes of the 1753 Act and towards the immediate reason: the moral panic over clandestine marriage.

3. CLANDESTINE MARRIAGE

It would be hard to find a better description of patriarchy's view of clandestine marriage than that provided by the early nineteenth-century novelist and historian Tobias Smollett (1830, vol. III, p. 100):

> The practice of solemnizing clandestine marriages, so prejudicial to the peace of families and so often productive of misery to the parties themselves thus united, was an evil that prevailed to such a degree as claimed the attention of the legislature. The sons and daughters of great and opulent families, before they had acquired knowledge and experience, or attained to the years of discretion, were everyday seduced in their affections, and inveigled into matches big with infamy and ruin; and these were greatly facilitated by the opportunities that occurred of being united instantaneously by the ceremony of marriage, in the first transport of passion, before the destined victim had time to cool or deliberate on the subject.

The law, which enabled marriage to be formed by the simple exchange of promises without preliminaries, was therefore seen as facilitating seduction or rashness to the disruption of 'great and opulent families'. There is no doubt that the idea of secrecy and elopement caught the imagination of genteel society which was increasingly accustomed to the idea of romantic marriage. Popular fiction abounded with references to secret weddings. Trevelyan suggests that a sham marriage enters into the plot of half the novels of the period (1881, p. 13):

> Numerous were the cases in which boys of rank had become the prey of infamous harpies, and girls with money or beauty had found that the services of a clergyman were employed as a cloak for plunder and seduction.

Much of the fiction from the period is now lost, but some is still read and performed today; the obvious example being Garrick's comedy, *The Clandestine Marriage*. The plot of Samuel Richardon's novel *The History of Sir Charles Grandison*, first published in 1754, is perhaps an even better illustration of the genre. Here, the beautiful and accomplished Harriet Byron is carried off by the arrogant and unscrupulous Sir Hargrave Pollexfen who attempts to carry through a secret marriage ceremony with her. Similarly, in Oliver Goldsmith's *The Vicar of Wakefield* the unprincipled ruffian Squire Thornhill

seduces the innocent sounding Olivia Primrose after a mock ceremony of marriage.

It is impossible to discover how many secret marriages within the
well-to-do *were* disastrous products of deceit and force and how many
were actually successful unions to which parents and 'society' eventually became reconciled. The fiction of the time may well have been
reflecting patriarchal ideas; perhaps partly because most writing
comes from within ruling ideologies and partly because the writers
often depended on sponsorship. Clandestine marriage seems to be
rather a neat example of a moral panic; a concept developed (in a
quite different context) by Stan Cohen. He says (1980, p. 9):

> Societies appear to be subject, every now and then, to periods of
> moral panic. A condition, episode, person or group of persons
> emerges to become defined as a threat to societal values and
> interests; its nature is presented in a stylized and stereotypical
> fashion by the mass media; the moral barricades are manned by
> editors, bishops, politicians and other right-thinking people; social-
> ly accredited experts pronounce their diagnoses and solutions;
> ways of coping are evolved or (more often) resorted to.

It is typical of a moral panic that it can be self-generating. Because
it concerns something topical, the behaviour is likely to be reported
(in our case, appear in popular fiction). The more it is reported the
more panic is generated as the deviancy is amplified (Hall, 1978,
chapter 3). Moral panics also tend to produce folk-devils, 'visible
reminders of what we should not be' (Cohen, 1980, p, 10). In the case
of clandestine marriages these are the ruffian and the harpy, even
though we do know of successful society marriages of the time which
began as elopements. The poet Charles Churchill, the Dukes of
Hamilton and Kingston and, as we will see later, the Secretary of
War, Henry Fox, all engaged in famous clandestine marriages
(Lecky, 1883, p. 491). Perhaps it is in the nature of moral panic that
the folk-devils are produced *in the face of* evidence that not all
participants behave in that way. Highly stylised villains are needed
around which concern can centre.

Of course, clandestine marriage with the implications of seduction
and fraud which it acquired was hardly the issue for the vast majority
of women and men in the eighteenth century who had little or no
property. The panic was therefore within a particular class and then,
to a certain extent, generalised. Furthermore, there had long been
concern about flexible marriage laws which, because they allowed

privacy, also allowed bigamy to take place. Many cases had come to light of respectable 'marriages' being vitiated by the discovery of an earlier precontract or secret marriage contracted in a hasty moment. These had considerable effects on the legitimacy of children and the devolution of property. Indeed, shortly before Hardwicke's Bill was introduced in the Lords, the House in its judicial capacity had heard such a case from Scotland (Cochrane v. Campbell, Paton's Cases I, p. 519 and Wilson and Shaw's Cases III, p. 135n). It seems to be this case that the Attorney-General of the day, Sir Dudley Ryder, referred to in the parliamentary debates on Hardwicke's Bill (Cobbett's Parliamentary History, vol. xv, p. 8):

> A gentleman had married a lady of family and fortune, had lived several years with her, yet after her death another woman laid claim to him as her husband by virtue of a marriage solemnized between them before his marriage with the lady, who he always acknowledged as his wife.

Attacks had been made on precontracts in England since at least 1540 and similar measures were introduced in many other European countries (Lasch, 1974, pp. 93–4). The English legislation was ineffective because it concentrated on penalising the clergy who officiated rather than impugning the marriage (Manchester, 1980, p. 364; MacQueen, 1858, p. 2 and Mueller, 1957, p. 558). What was needed in order for sweeping legislation to be introduced was a trigger; something that could draw together and orchestrate concern. That trigger was provided by Fleet marriages.

The Fleet was the prison in which prisoners for debt were confined. Because accommodation was insufficient, those prisoners who could give security for their appearance when summoned were permitted to take lodgings nearby. One class of prisoner likely to be trusted was clergymen. From the environs of the Fleet, clergymen plied their trade of conducting marriage services which, because they involved the exchange of consents to marry, had legal effect. Fleet marriages have been well-documented by a number of writers (see, for example, Howard, 1904, vol. I, p. 438). Smollett's account is typically colourful (1830, p. 100):

> . . . a band of profligate miscreants, the refuse of the clergy, dead to every sentiment of virtue, abandoned to all sense of decency and decorum, for the most part prisoners for debt or delinquency, and indeed the very outcasts of human society, who hovered about the

verge of the Fleet-prison to intercept customers, plying like porters for employment, performed the ceremony of marriage without licence or question, in cellars, garrets, or alehouses, to the scandal of religion, and the disgrace of that order which they professed.

The most enterprising of these miscreants seems to have been the Reverend Alexander Keith. He is said to have made a very 'bishopric of revenue' from clandestine marriages and it was said in Parliament that he had married on an average 6000 couples every year (Lecky, 1883, p. 490). As a last fling, on the day before Lord Hardwicke's Act came into effect he married sixty-one couples and, vowing eternal vengeance on bishops, bought several acres of land for burials and threatened to underbury them all (Baker, 1977, p. 48). It is estimated that on that last day 217 Fleet marriages were conducted in all (Haw, 1952, p. 147). One should remember that these irregular marriages were not only valid for ecclesiastical purposes, the civil authorities regarded the presence of a clergyman sufficient for property and legitimacy consequences (Brown, 1981, p. 118), although there is a suggestion that laymen may have dressed up as priests (Howard, 1904, vol. i, p. 438).

Despite the fact that clandestine marriages had been of concern to the authorities for so long (and long before the Fleet episode the Tower of London chaplains conducted a similar trade [Brown, 1981, p. 119]) the structural changes I referred to in the previous section meant that the Fleet symbolised the threat to patriarchal control at a time when that control was both more necessary and more resisted. Even amongst those who would later be called the middle class, whose interests were not so directly threatened, there was an outburst of indignation about the general debasement of marriage (Lasch, 1974, p. 95). The age was perceived to be one of unparalleled depravity in the eyes of the growing class of merchants and tradesmen, whose domestic lives were already resembling what we now know as the Victorian family (Porter, 1982, p. 186). So the conditions were right for fundamental change. To understand the form that the change took, it is necessary to look at the nature of the rulers.

4. THE LAW-MAKERS

If Lord Hardwicke had a likeable side to his character it has been firmly hidden from history. Born Philip Yorke, the son of a Dover attorney, he rapidly rose to public office as a lawyer. He became Solicitor-General in 1720, at the age of 29, and eventually, by way of the offices of Attorney-General and Lord Chief Justice, the Lord Chancellor. He has been described as 'the quintessence of Whiggism' and 'the old spider of the law' (Plucknett, 1940, p. 623). Through bribery and patronage he skilfully acquired both a fortune and a reputation for probity. Quite how he came by the latter is all the more amazing when one learns that as Lord Chancellor he maintained his position as the only Law Lord in order to preserve decisions he had made as Lord Chief Justice. One does not know whether Lord Campbell, in his *Lives of the Lord Chancellors* (1846, vol. v, p. 49), is being serious when he pays tribute to Hardwicke for the luminous perspicuity of his judgments in that none of his decisions was ever upset!

E.P. Thompson says that Hardwicke's 'entire career was marked by contempt for the rabble, severity in handling rioters and rebels (whether turnpike protesters in the West of England or Highland clansmen) and for the liberty of the press he can hardly be said to have had any respect whatsoever' (Thompson, 1977, p. 208). His disgust for the poor is well documented. In 1737 he was complaining that 'the people are always jealous of those in power, and mighty apt to believe every piece of scandal or reproach that is thrown upon them' (Cobbett's Parliamentary History, vol. ix, col. 1295). He was the architect of numerous capital statutes passed during the 1730s, attributing their necessity to 'the degeneracy of human nature' (Hay, 1977, p. 20). In his judicial capacity he added subtle refinements to his own statutes by, for example, ordering a Cornish rioter's body to hang in chains; an order he only respited when told that insurrection would follow.

But Hardwicke was not alone in his view of the common people. He simply personified the new breed of ruler. If the period 1780–1820 saw the formation of class consciousness amongst the new working class, the preceding forty years saw the emergence of a distinctive ruling class ideology. Any surfacing of popular discontent was liable to be attributed to envy and jealousy (Malcolmson, 1981, p. 109). Patricians grew increasingly snooty about the 'vulgar world' and popular customs and festivities came in for particular obloquy. This hostility to the way of life of ordinary people had three closely related aspects to it; political, economic and ideological.

I referred in the previous chapter to custom being a source of self-defence in a highly unequal society; as one of the ways in which power was disciplined and concessions enjoyed. Disturbances were increasingly seen in the eighteenth century as the product of concerted collective action and the squirearchy was well aware that focal points for local solidarity, such as customs, had to be eroded. Storch notes that popular culture was conceived by the middle classes as a set of beliefs and behaviour which could be threatening to public order; the most obvious one being local wakes (Storch, 1982, p. 1). So custom was seen as an impediment to the effective exercise of power.

Economically, village festivities, involving (as they did) heavy drinking, hindered the establishment of new norms of work and social conduct. Porter quotes one village parson condemning the celebration of wakes because 'with lower sort of people, especially in the manufacturing villages, the return of the wake never fails to produce a week, at least, of idleness, intoxication and riot' (1982, p. 171). It is reasonable to assume that marriage and disorder were tied together in the minds of rulers at this time. The popular 'big wedding' involved considerable public celebration and some mock violence, if not actual violence. Whilst these were dying out by this time the perception of them may not have been.

This leads us to ideological reasons why common behaviour might be so despised. Superstitions and beliefs (which abounded in the context of marriage rituals) conflicted with the 'rationalism' of the new political economy. For that rationalism to take hold, the rulers' world view had to be embraced throughout the social order. Deriving particularly from the work of the Italian Marxist Antonio Gramsci, the term 'hegemony' has come to mean more than simple political preponderance by one class over another. The rulers' *culture* must be accepted by a significant proportion of the population, as well as their political and economic institutions. Raymond Williams suggests that the ability to impose 'ways of seeing' is crucial in societies where government depends, in the last resort, on consent rather than coercion (Williams, 1976, p. 118 and 1980, pp. 37–40). Whig rule in an England (and Wales) without a police force or flexible militia depended on popular consent; albeit a consent manipulated through the majesty, mercy and occasional justice of the criminal law (Hay, 1977, chapter 1).

Christopher Lasch has said that the Act 'should be viewed as, amongst other things, another dose of what R.H. Tawney called "the new medicine of poverty". It was one of a whole series of measures by means of which eighteenth-century reformers attempted to bring about "a general reformation of manners amongst the lower sort of people" ' (Lasch, 1974, p. 105). I am not sure that it is correct to imply that the *proposal* to abolish informal marriage was specifically motivated by hegemonic considerations but it does seem that those considerations played a part in rallying support for the measure and muting the opposition.

An examination of the debates in Parliament may make this clearer. There was only the faintest opposition to the measure in the House of Lords. Its passage there was predictable because they were the class whose reproduction relied so much on control over marriage. Most of the previous attempts to regulate clandestine marriage (1677, 1685, 1689, 1691, 1695, 1711 and 1735) had passed in the Lords but failed in the Commons (Trumbach, 1978, p. 102). For this reason I concentrate on the debates in the Commons. Perhaps one should say at the outset that one has to take the participants at face value and assume they mean what they are recorded as saying. It is quite possible that personal animosities distorted the genuineness of some of the opposition. Further, the spectre of Jacobitism so haunted the political life of the period that suspicions and recriminations were likely to be carried over to matters which were relatively non-party (Clark, 1982, p. 39).

The arguments in support of the Bill can be disposed of briefly because we have considered at length the two major issues; seduction of young heirs and heiresses, and later marriages being vitiated by the discovery of an earlier informal one. The opening remarks of the Attorney-General, Sir Dudley Ryder, who introduced the Bill in the Commons, were brief and to the point. He asked (Cobbett, vol. xv, p. 3):

> How often have we known the heir of a good family seduced, and engaged in a clandestine marriage, perhaps with a common strumpet? How often have we known a rich heiress carried off by a man of low birth, or perhaps by an infamous sharper?

And, although neither he nor anyone else could answer that question, John Bond found it astonishing that anyone should oppose such an 'eminently sensible measure' (Cobbett, p. 42).

Opposition there was, however, and at the cost of some simplification I group the objections under three main headings.

(a)   Social Mobility within the Propertied Classes

Two vocal antagonists, Robert Nugent and Charles Townshend, saw the Act as an aristocratic plot to prevent commoners marrying into their ranks. According to the former (Cobbett, pp. 14–15):

> When a young commoner makes addresses to a rich heiress he has no friend but his superior merit, and that little deity called love, whose influence over a young lady always decreases as she increases in years; for by the time she comes of age, pride and ambition seize possession of her breast likewise, and banishes from thence the little deity called love, or if he preserves a corner for his friend, it is only to introduce him as a gallant, not as a husband. Therefore I prophecy that if this Bill passes into law, no commoner will ever marry a rich heiress, unless his father be a minister of state, nor will a peer's eldest son marry the daughter of a commoner, unless she be a rich heiress.

In a similar vein, Charles Townshend asked (Cobbett, p. 69):

> Are new shackles to be forged to keep young men of abilities from rising to a level of their elder brothers?

The latter is obviously alluding to primogeniture and this suggests a belief that seduction was the alternative open to younger sons (such as himself, incidentally). Mahon remarks wryly that 'the Bill proved no such obstruction in the way of Townshend's own career. Only a year afterwards he espoused a wealthy Dowager from the House of Buccleuch—the Countess of Dalkeith' (Mahon, 1858, p. 27).

Whilst Trevelyan describes Townshend's rhetorical appeal as 'pathetic' (1881, p. 14), the remarks should be seen in their context. The agrarian revolution, which was eradicating feudal traditions, abolishing feudal tenures and commercialising agriculture, had led to a resurgence of aristocratic power; temporarily halting the ascendance of the middle class (Lasch, 1974, p. 102). It is quite likely, then, that commoners might be suspicious of the measure. Furthermore, it underlines one of the arguments of this chapter that the restructuring of agriculture along capitalist lines was having profound effects at the political level.

Henry Fox, the main opponent of the Bill, converted the arguments of Nugent and Townshend into constitutional language. By preventing commoners from marrying into their ranks, this might increase the elective power of the nobility which 'will be of more danger to our constitution than ever their military power was'. Continuing in this vein he said (Cobbett, p. 70):

> . . . for a factious majority of the other House, having by means of their elective power, got a majority in this, will soon force the Crown to put the whole military power of the kingdom into their hands.

As we shall see shortly, however, Fox's remarks on the future of the constitution may not have been untinged by the origins of his own notorious marriage.

(b) Individualism and Romantic Love

The mid-eighteenth century marked a surge in what we now call individualism. Some historians argue that English individualism can be traced back to medieval times when land was freely alienable and ownership vested in the head of the family rather than the family itself (Macfarlane, 1978; Plucknett, 1940, p. 466). The individualism exhibited in the mid-eighteenth century, however, was a more ordered collection of ideas. On government and wealth, these ideas were shortly to be systemised in the political economy of Adam Smith. On social life, they are typified by the growing attraction of romantic love as the basis of marriage.

As a general proposition, one can argue that those who favoured the Bill belonged to, or identified with, the landed wing of the ruling class. The threat posed by romantic love to their marriage practices required strong measures (even if, at an individual level, many of their own marriages were increasingly the result of personal choice [Trumbach, 1978, p. 113]). On the other hand, those who identified with the merchant or trade wing of the governing elite were more likely to be sympathetic to affective marriage and therefore oppose the Bill.

Several reasons can be suggested for this broad division. First, the interests of the merchant class were less threatened by the idea of companionate marriage. Second, it provided opportunities to add social status to their wealth by enabling them to marry into a title (although the Stones' research, 1984, indicates that the opportunities might have been scarcer than they believed). Third, the way they made their money was through contractual, arm's length bargaining. They may therefore have been more likely to see the world as comprising autonomous, free-willing, individuals and the marriage contract was not to be distinguished from any other form of contract. A quotation from Horace Walpole, who sat in the Commons as a Whig from 1741 to 1767 (and who opposed the Bill) serves as a good example of this perspective. In his *Memoirs* he recalled (1847, vol. I, p. 340):

It was amazing in a country where liberty gives choice, where trade and money confer equality, and where facility of marriage had always been supposed to produce populousness—it was amazing to see a law promulgated that cramped inclination, that discountenanced matrimony, and that seemed to annex as sacred privileges to birth, as could be devised in the proudest, poorest little Italian principality.

Henry Fox epitomised the (eighteenth-century) idea of free love. At the age of 43, when Secretary at War, he fell in love with the daughter of the Duke and Duchess of Richmond, Lady Caroline Lennox. The Duke refused his daughter's hand to Fox (he was already looking for a more eligible suitor). In the early month of May 1744, in Trevelyan's words (1881, pp. 8–9):

. . . the town was convulsed by the intelligence that the lovers had settled the matter by a secret wedding, which in those days was a much less arduous operation than at present. The sensation was instant and tremendous. At the opera the news ran along the front boxes exactly like fire in a train of gunpowder. It was said at the time that more noise could hardly have been made if the Princess Caroline had gone off with her dancing master.

Trevelyan's account illustrates nicely the point that clandestine marriage was both outrageous and titillating. Lady Caroline's parents remained obdurate until 1748 when the appearance of a grandson (Charles James Fox) melted their opposition.

The fact that the Foxes' marriage was extremely happy, despite their virtual ostracism in its early years, clearly contributed to his fury at seeing clandestine marriages attacked in Hardwicke's Bill. He stood forth as the champion of the oppressed lover declaring that it was cruel to force upon the country a measure which, from the first word to the last, was dictated by aristocratic pride and heartlessness. A bitter feud developed between him and Hardwicke which at one stage required the King's intervention.

At a general level, then, the split over the Bill can be regarded as a split within the ruling classes; the proponents representing patriarchy and landed property, the opponents representing (relative) freedom of youth and merchant capital. It was not, however, a complete split along party lines. The main disputants actually all occupied the same Treasury Benches on the Whig side. Further, the generalisation is clouded by arguments which men like Fox, Nugent and Townshend adduced concerning the effect the Act would have upon the poor. Whilst such men, politically, were nearer to what we now know as nineteenth-century Whig-Liberals, in another sense they appeared to be speaking for an older tradition, rooted in popular practice (Lasch, 1974, p. 104). Whether or not they were genuine in their concern for the poor is for the reader to judge.

(c) The Effect of the Act upon the Poor

The opponents of the Bill speculated on the effect it might have upon the propertyless classes. Fox felt that it would discourage marriage amongst the poor on a number of grounds. First, it would make marriage more expensive, because the Parson's fee would have to be paid. Second, the compulsory four week period of notice would give time for a change of mind and allow the lusty swain's ardour to cool. Third, the compulsory register would deter those who were illiterate (Cobbett, p. 70). Colonel George Haldane pointed out that the attractions of Fleet marriages for many people were that they were private (and there was a widespread objection to banns) and they were cheap. Nugent, perhaps showing greater insight than Fox, referred to the four week delay and asked (Cobbett, p. 12):

> Would a labouring man who can by hard labour earn but a little more than is necessary for supporting himself in what he may think an elegant manner: would such a man, I say, incumber himself with a wife and child, if he was directed by nothing but the dictates of wisdom and foresight?

Fears over the discouragement of marriage were not born, however, out of concern for the emotional development of the poor. Rather, it was thought that the population might fall. According to Fox, without a 'continual supply of industrious and laborious poor, no nation can long exist, which supply can only be got by promoting marriage amongst such people' (Cobbett, p. 70).

Perhaps the only remark that can be viewed without excessive cynicism is that by Nugent concerning what I have referred to earlier as processual marriage. Nugent correctly saw that the removal of backing from customs whereby a marriage only became binding upon conception would be dangerous to the girl (and the rate-payer). He said (Cobbett, p. 17):

> A young woman is but too apt by nature to trust to the honour of the man she loves, and to admit him to her bed upon a solemn promise to marry her. Surely the moral obligation is as binding as if they have been actually married: but you are by this Bill to declare it null and void.

Even this observation grossly simplifies the sophisticated marriage customs of many ordinary people and Nugent was alone in alluding to them. In my view, it is the *absence* of reflection on the impact of the Act upon the population which is as significant as any express reference to it. Some of the participants in the debate must have had some idea of what really happened out there, if only because *noblesse oblige* required them to have some involvement in significant rites of passage amongst their flock. To the extent that the rulers actually knew about the customs of the people, they were held in contempt. They were certainly not to be factors in decisions which affected the transmission of property and social mobility amongst the élite.

(e) Other Points of Opposition

If there was any genuine concern with women's rights evinced by the opponents of the Bill, I would be happy to discuss it. All of the language is informed by assumed notions of gender relations. Virtually all references to women were in the context of sexuality and physical attraction. It would have been unthinkable to have discussed the substantive nature of marriage: the Act was about entry into marriage rather than its consequences. Townshend alleged that 'the highest bloom of a woman's beauty is from sixteen to twenty-one: it is then that a young woman of little or no fortune has the best chance of disposing of herself to advantage in marriage'. 'Shall we', he asked, 'make it impossible for her to do so without the consent of an indigent and mercenary father?' (Cobbett, p. 59).

We are told that the Church was not keen on the Act. Whilst individual clergymen will have been heartened by a sharp upturn in business, far-sighted ecclesiastical politicians would have been less happy. Despite the fact that marriage in a church was now compulsory, the Act was the first major attempt by civil authorities to make the formation of marriage a secular matter (Lecky, 1883, p. 493; Weeks, 1981, p. 83). Hardwicke himself was anti-clerical and explicitly set himself against an extensive view of Church powers (Clark, 1985, pp. 380 and 302) and we can assume that he intended to use the church as part of a registration system rather than concede any real ground to it.

5. CONCLUSION

Whereas in chapter 2 I looked at the marriage practices of the poor and the impact of economic change upon them, I have tried here to present a parallel account in respect of the upper echelons. Both chapters have contained largely static analyses. I have tried to bring out the relevance of class, property and generation in explaining why differing practices over marriage entry existed and why some behaviour was at least tolerated, if not condoned. Apart from referring to the way in which some customary forms were designed to help women enforce marriage, or escape from it, and to some beliefs about maintaining separate property, I have found it more difficult to analyse matters from a gender perspective. This may partly be due to the relative dearth of literature for this period written by and about women who are taken, almost axiomatically, as being hidden from history. It might also be the case that local social structures had changed so little that women were firmly locked into position; that the gains made over marriage entry were the most that they could make. As the pace of change increases, with proletarianisation and urbanisation shaking up those social structures, it becomes easier to talk about women and men rather than 'people'.

Some aspects of the dynamic relationship between popular practice and State prescription, between private and public ordering, between social and legal normative orders, have come out. On the other hand, the real game of cat and mouse between law and social practice now began in earnest because the law had stamped a uniform and inflexible definition of marriage. In my argument, the history of marriage law is a gradual, if ambiguous, retreat from that position and it began with the introduction of civil marriage.

4 Marriage and the Law 1754–1927: The State Retreats?

1. INTRODUCTION

This chapter deals with the period between Lord Hardwicke's Act 1753 and the demise of the 'unmarried wife' in employment insurance legislation in 1927. The most important statutory change was the Civil Marriage Act 1836 and the chapter is mainly concerned with that Act. I omit discussion of some legislation on marriage entry, although one should note in passing that Hardwicke's Act itself was repealed and re-enacted in the Marriage Act 1823. The thrust of the 1823 Act was to make the validity of marriages in breach of statutory requirements depend on the parties' knowledge and intention so that mistakes in the formalities did not render the marriage void. I also omit discussion of major changes in what is now called 'family law'. The introduction of judicial divorce in 1857 and separate property rights for married women in 1870–82 were major changes in the *consequences* of formal marriage. They have been fully dealt with from feminist perspectives (Holcombe, 1983; Stetson, 1982) and the focus of this book is specifically on marriage entry. Overall the period is one of a gradual retreat by the State. The reasons for the retreat, and the terms on which it took place, show the relationship between legal and social practice in altering the boundaries of marriage.

2. THE CIVIL MARRIAGE ACT 1836

The Civil Marriage Act 1836 made two major innovations into the marriage law of England and Wales. It allowed purely secular ceremonies of marriage before the District Superintendent-Registrar and it allowed the registration of Dissenters' places of worship 'for the solemnization of marriages therein'. The latter are still properly called civil marriages because the necessary preliminaries were the new civil ones and they could only take place if a District Registrar was present in the building. The Church of England retained the

48

exclusive right to conduct religious marriage ceremonies in the strict sense. This brief survey of the 1836 Act is sufficient to show that remarkable changes of attitude must have taken place over eighty years or so. The apparent tolerance and latitude of the new measure, which seemed to cater for most people's marriage preferences, contrast sharply with the rigid provisions of Lord Hardwicke's Act. In this chapter I will try to account for what appears to be a radical change of direction.

The period 1754–1836 was an unusually turbulent one in social history and it is probably impossible to present in one account all the strands which intertwined to produce circumstances in which formal marriage law could be relaxed. In keeping with my attempt to prioritise issues of class, gender and generation I try to extract developments which had a direct bearing on them. Because the argument is complex, it might help the reader if I present a simplified version at the outset. The economic changes in the period, collectively referred to as the Industrial Revolution, had profound effects on social and political life. Two particularly significant ones were urbanisation and growing religious dissent. These related phenomena highlighted the oppressive nature of enforced Anglican marriage; a system which had been imposed on a predominantly rural society where marriage was a central institution in the transmission of wealth and power. Hence there was pressure from below for some relaxation of the law. The reasons why those on high granted the concession and why it took the form it did are threefold. First, civil marriage was seen as an important element in a comprehensive system of births, deaths and marriage registration; a system increasingly necessary with the formation of a modern State. Second, religious nonconformism was seen to be beneficial to the social order as it brought a sobering influence to bear on the working classes. Third, the open flouting of Hardwicke's Act threatened to undermine the whole basis of State regulation of marriage, and legitimacy had to be restored to the law.

(a) Economic, Social and Political Change 1754–1836

(i) Economic Change

Economic historians may differ over the usefulness of the expression Industrial Revolution but, for our purposes, between 1753 and 1836 two important processes accelerated which had profound impact on social life generally and marriage practices in particular. These are the extension of wage labour and the shift away from agriculture to manufacturing.

The dominant image of the Industrial Revolution is one of self-employed smallholders being forced off the land and flocking to the new towns and cities in search of factory employment. This image is an over-simplification, however. First, as I argued in chapter 2, much of the family's income in the mid-eighteenth century already derived from wage-labour on the land and work put out by manufacturers. The family was, therefore, adapting itself to new economic conditions prior to industrialisation. The 'domestic mode of production', in Scott and Tilly's phrase (1975), was already in decline. Events in the second half of the century merely increased this process. Second, in 1801, agriculture, forestry and fishing was still the largest category of employment, occupying 35.9 per cent of the workforce whilst manufacturing, mining and industry employed 29.7 per cent. The positions were, however, reversed by 1841 (Tranter, 1981, p. 206). Third, a distinction should be drawn between manufacturing and the factory system. E.P. Thompson has argued that we should not overstate the extent to which the new mechanised place of production replaced early forms of manufacture driven by water-power. With the exception of the cotton industry, trades adapted quite slowly to the possibilities offered by steam power (Thompson, 1968, pp. 207 *et seq.*). Thompson cautions against too much emphasis upon the newness of cotton because it can lead to an under-estimation of the continuity of political and cultural traditions in the making of working class communities (1968, p. 21).

This last remark is particularly relevant to a study of the family over the period. As we will see, marriage and family practices of early industrial England and Wales were adaptations of older traditions. The relative mobility of the new workers, not yet tied to a single factory job, is an important element in new types of informal marriage. Whereas older forms may often have had the quality of trial marriage, the new ones explicitly recognised that one or both of the partners might have to move on in search of work and it had to be publicly understood that departure in these circumstances was not desertion.

(ii)   Social Change
The key aspects of social change isolated here are urbanisation, class formation, adaptation of the family, the rise of nonconformism and

the revolutionary amendment to the Poor Law. Taken together, they may help explain the pressure from below for some alternative to Lord Hardwicke's Act.

The most visible manifestation of the new social order was the growth of industrial towns in the north of England and the midlands. In 1801, there were only fifteen towns with over 20000 inhabitants; by 1851 there were sixty-three (Rose, 1981, p. 257). In 1831, the number of people living in rural areas still marginally outnumbered those in urban districts but by 1851, according to the Census, for the first time in history just over half the population in England and Wales was living in towns and cities (Harrison, 1979, pp. 26–7). The new urban environment helps explain a more plebeian, secular flavour to some of the emerging informal marriage practices. The private exchange of rings replaces the more public rustic ritual of jumping the broom. Furthermore, unprecedented loose community control enabled the young in some areas to engage in cohabitation and free association which had been impossible in the rural homelands.

The combined effect of the changing mode of production and the concentration of the population into towns and cities was the creation of new forms of class consciousness. Whilst pre-industrial society could still be depicted as hierarchical, or pyramid-like, industrialisation brought a new rank ordering which replaced the old balance of rank and degree with a society divided horizontally by class. This gradually brought with it a distinctive sense of collective identity which permeated all social practices; not simply those connected with work and wage bargaining. Urbanisation was equally important, however, in producing a distinctive middle class—perhaps more distinctive than today—particularly in cities such as Manchester and Birmingham (Harrison, 1979, p. 128). The new middle class demanded reform of institutions and the reduction of aristocratic and landed privilege in economic political and religious spheres; demands which were mediated through the growing provincial press. The middle class were instrumental in bringing about the Poor Law Amendment Act 1834, which was structurally linked to the idea of civil marriage. Their approach to government, central and local, was bureaucratic in the Weberian sense and it is no accident that the Marriage Act 1836 was passed together with an ideal type of bureaucratic measure, the Births and Deaths Registration Act. The middle class also produced evangelical reformers, liberal philanthropists, as well as hard-headed capitalists. Their concern to 'moralise' the working classes included a desire to impose their own family form. This is an important factor in amendments to family law in the nineteenth century generally.

The whole subject of class is, of course, problematic in historical and sociological scholarship and I am taking a rather simple view of it here. Classes, as Thompson says, are not heavenly hosts to be 'marshalled, sent on manoeuvres and marched up and down whole centuries' (Thompson, 1978, p. 85). They comprise people who often behave differently than their ascribed world-view would suggest. I hope that the approach taken here, however, is sufficient to base the discussion of the hegemonic tendencies described later.

For convenience, evasive and alternative marriage practices are dealt with in a separate section of this chapter. It is appropriate here, however, to mention changes in the family generally over this period. The information we have for the late eighteenth and early nineteenth centuries is fragmented and is often gleaned from literature the specific object of which is not the family. In any event, generalisations are highly suspect. Industrialisation took place in different forms and at different rates throughout England and Wales. Furthermore, immigrant workers from the countryside brought with them their own traditions which coloured the practices of particular urban areas (Anderson, 1980, p. 78 and, generally, 1974).

In chapter 2 I mentioned the importance of customary practices and festivities in re-affirming identity with place and class. There is considerable evidence that this attachment to ceremony and rituals was transported to the new towns. In particular, old family and kinship practices were preserved. Jane Humphries argues that the nineteenth-century working class was intimately aware of the family's importance as an economic support unit and was therefore suspicious of the Poor Law Amendment Act 1834 because workhouses were seen as attempts to break up poor families (Humphries, 1977, p. 25). Raymond Williams suggests that the use of 'brother' and 'sister' to express class affiliation, as in trade union membership, derived mainly from the newly heightened sense of the family's importance in early industrial England (1976, p. 111) although one suspects that the terms also had their roots in nonconformist language. One should also remember that much migration to the towns may not have involved great distances. A high proportion of immigrants made a journey of ten miles or less (Redford, 1926) so that contacts with friends and relatives may not have been entirely lost. A further factor in the retention of a strong sense of family identity may have been the practice, in some employments, of the whole family working together. Hall notes that this was common in cotton mills until about 1850 (Hall, 1982, p. 25).

Change there was, however. The age of first marriage fell. In some areas quite dramatically. Whereas in the first half of the eighteenth century the mean age of first marriages for males and females was 27.5 and 26.2, respectively, a century later it had dropped to 25.3 and 23.4. These figures might not appear startling but, according to Gillis (1985, p. 110), the fall in the mean age of first marriage was the single most important factor in the surge of population growth. One obvious reason for the fall in marriage age was the ease of access to marriage. In closed agricultural communities marriage was commonly delayed until a small-holding or other resources were available to support the family but the presence of factory employment offered greater independence to the young. In particular, industrial towns offered single women the prospect of financial autonomy and a wider choice of marriage partners (Banks, 1967, p. 277). Gillis suggests that being accustomed to their own wages enabled young men and women to bargain with their parents and masters. It also caused them to regard all relationships, including the conjugal, as products of a certain give-and-take; not as something bestowed or unalterable (1985, p. 173).

One source of ideology which stressed the preservation of the family was Methodism. In 1767 there were about 24000 Methodists. By 1796 there were over 77000 (Porter, 1982, p. 193) and this had almost doubled to 150000 by 1811 (Hobsbawm, 1964, p. 23). In 1830 the figure was just short of a quarter of a million. Methodism was also regionalised (Rule, 1982) and so in some areas it was a major denomination. Methodism performed a dual role as the religion both of the exploited and exploiters. For the former it provided a sense of community and satisfied (and was the product of) the psychic needs of a disrupted society. At its radical edge, it provided legitimation for collective action such as machine-breaking. In Charlotte Brontë's *Shirley*, for example, the Luddite riots take place alongside a surge of dissenting religious practices in an industrial village. Methodism was also attractive to the young on the move, providing emotional stability and, perhaps, accommodation on arrival (Gillis, 1974, p. 81).

On the other hand, Methodism benefited the exploiters. Halevy's assertion that Methodism averted political revolution in 1811 has been attacked as overstating the influence of 150000 English and

Welsh Methodists in a population of ten million (Morris, 1979, p. 68) but, at the very least, it provided a sobering influence. In the first place it stressed the value of work discipline. In 1787 the first Robert Peel wrote 'I have left most of my works in Lancashire under the management of Methodists, and they serve me excellently well' (Tyerman, 1870, vol. II, p. 499). Second, Methodism stressed the stability of home and family and the need for obedience in children (Jarrett, 1976, p. 69). It was therefore a 'moralising' influence in the new factories and mills which were constantly being indicted as centres of gross sexual immorality. It is perhaps because of its emphasis on discipline and the home that Methodism was attractive to a substantial section of the middle class as well. Whilst Hansard reports do not carry the religious affiliation of MPs, it is clear from the debates over the Marriage Bill that certain Members were spokesmen for dissenting religion.

This dual role which Methodism performed is important to our understanding of pressures for civil marriage. The contempt with which Anglican church forms were treated generally by dissenters was heightened in the context of marriage. Lord Hardwicke's Act required them to attend an Anglican church to be married (although we have no idea how many actually did) and the publicity procedures offended the dissenting notion of marriage as a private contract. One can see, therefore, how demands would grow for the registration of dissenting chapels as buildings for the solemnisation of marriage. Equally, one can see how Parliament felt that this might be a concession worth making.

Finally under the heading of social change is the Poor Law Amendment Act 1834. Since the sixteenth century, each parish in England and Wales had been statutorily responsible for the relief, mainly in the form of income supplement, of its destitute members. In 1601 the system was codified and provision made for the election of an overseer in each parish to administer it. During the eighteenth century the Poor Law came in for constant criticism. Scores of pamphlets, many of them penned in country rectories, appeared suggesting either total abolition or its drastic reform (Poynter, 1969). By the early nineteenth century two specific criticisms stood out (both of which have a depressingly modern ring): the alleged tendency of the system to promote over-population through reckless marriage and the alleged erosion of work discipline by providing something for nothing.

In 1832 a Royal Commission was set up under the chairmanship of the Benthamite utilitarian Edwin Chadwick to investigate 'the administration and operation of the Poor Laws' and this resulted in the Poor Law Amendment Act 1834. The Act passed the task of poor relief from parish authorities to Boards of elected guardians under central supervision and control. Any relief given to the able-bodied poor was to be in such a form as to make their condition less desirable (or 'eligible') than that of the poorest independent labourer. To achieve this, workhouses were set up with a strict regime of low diet and hard work. When married couples entered the workhouse husbands and wives were segregated to prevent pauper brats from being brought into the world. Under the infamous bastardy clauses, unmarried mothers could no longer bring affiliation actions against putative fathers and liability for an illegitimate child was firmly placed upon the mother.

The 1834 Act is relevant to the introduction of civil marriage in both structural and ideological ways. Structurally, the administrative framework it set up (such as Boards of Guardians, Clerks and Auditors) was later used as the basis for the whole system of births, deaths and marriage registration. This, I will argue, was a precondition of the introduction of civil marriage. Furthermore, under the Marriage Act 1836, notice of impending marriage was to be read to three weekly meetings of the Board of Guardians which gave them control over the marriage prospects of the poor. Two years later, the marriage registrars were drawn from the ranks of Poor Law officials and this gave them the chance to insist upon marriage as a condition of relief (remembering that they themselves officiated over the ceremony). The Poor Law Amendment Act, the Births and Deaths Registration Act and the Marriage Act therefore form a logical, if unholy, trinity.

Ideologically, the deliberations of the Royal Commission provided the occasion for the formulation of new utilitarian ideas about marriage and the family; ideologies which informed much of the marriage legislation in the nineteenth century. 'Improvident marriages' were said to lead to population crises and a drain on public funds. For example, one of the Commissioners, Mr Villiers, observed that large families were 'considered to be a source of profit. Women object to marrying until they are pregnant' (Villiers, 1833, p. 161). Pausing briefly there, it is likely that the worthy Mr Villiers was misreading the nature of the popular custom of not marrying until *after* conception. This illustrates the remoteness of the country's rulers from the marriage practices of the poor. It may also have produced an undesired result. By taking affiliation proceedings out of the reach of the mother it removed an important lever which had previously been used to force the man to marry her should he prove reluctant (Gill, 1977, p. 215). In attempting to confine women's sexuality to the marriage bed, the Act may actually have been self-defeating.

(iii) Political Change

Most of the preceding discussion of social change in this period suggested reasons why there might be pressure from below for a secular form of marriage. The Poor Law Amendment Act 1834 provides a convenient bridge to the political reasons why civil marriage might be desirable from above. I isolate three developments here; the beginnings of a modern state bureaucracy, electoral reform to take account of the newly elected powerful middle class and the beginnings of an explicit secular movement to improve the morals of the working class. All three contribute to the political environment within which civil marriage should be situated.

The second half of the eighteenth century saw the gradual replacement of 'Old Corruption', with its bribery, patronage and 'channels of influence' (Thompson, 1968, p. 322), by a recognisably bureaucratic system of government. Bureaucratic is used here in the Weberian ideal-typical sense as involving fixed areas of official jurisdiction governed by laws and regulations, officers organised on the basis of a clear hierarchy of authority and appointed on the basis of technical qualifications and administration based on written documents (Weber, 1964, pp. 329–41). An agrarian social formation based on local forms of patronage and a relatively settled population was being transformed into a mechanised, urban, industrial social formation based on national markets of employment and a relatively mobile population. This transformation required new methods of control and regulation. During this time we see the origins of a permanent civil service, the institution of budgets, the Consolidated Fund (1787) and the Exchequer Loans Commission (1793). The 1830s in particular saw a surge of modernisation influenced by utilitarians such as Bentham and Chadwick. In the period between the Reform Act 1832 and the Crimean War in 1854 the machinery of central and local administration was refashioned, a modern police force was established, new public hygiene and education services were brought in and a new start was made in the public inspection and control of private economic enterprises (Finer, 1952, p. 1).

A precondition of the programmatic planning required by the new order was accurate data about the population; its size, geographical concentration and age distribution. The story behind the introduction of a national Census neatly encapsulates the period. The first proposal for a national Census seems to have been made in 1753 (the same year as Hardwicke's Act was passed). It was vigorously opposed in the House of Commons. William Thornton of Cattal in Yorkshire, representing the land-owning interest, declared that the Census would give valuable information to enemies abroad and at home. The latter, he explained, were 'place-men and tax masters'. Turning the issue into one of State control over free-born Englishmen, he declared (Cobbett's *Parliamentary History*, vol. XIV, col. 1318):

> As to myself, I hold this project to be totally subversive of the last remains of English liberty . . . If any officer, by whatever authority, should demand of me an account of the number and circumstances of my family, I would refuse it; and if he persisted in the affront, I would order my servants to give him the discipline of the horse-pond.

In the face of opposition like this, the proposal was dropped. By 1800, however, the same idea passed through the Houses of Parliament amidst almost universal acclaim. Dealing with the period between the two Census debates Jarrett remarks that both 'in their original unaccountability and in the final resignation to being counted, the English bore witness to a progress from turbulence to regimentation which influenced every circumstance of their lives during this half-century (Jarrett, 1976, p. 33).

The Census is relevant to this study other than as an illustration of change, however. The defects in the first three Censuses created pressure for an improved registration system. These Censuses had relied upon parish registers which recorded baptisms rather than births, burials rather than deaths and formal marriages (meaning those according to Anglican rites). Increasingly these statistics were unreliable. Alienation from the established Church meant that more and more dissenters developed their own rites on birth, death and marriage. What was necessary was a more comprehensive *civil* system of registration on which to base the Census and provide updating information between Census years. The Poor Law Amendment Act provided the ideal framework onto which a registration system could be grafted. This was not entirely accidental because there is evidence that Chadwick had intended all along that the new

Poor Law ought to become the basis of a single set of multi-purpose authorities (Finer, 1952, p. 125). The whole country was now divided into poor law regions (called Unions) and so there was a ready-made network of overseers, clerks and accountants from whom the new registrars could be drawn.

The Births and Deaths Registration Bill was introduced into the House of Commons by Lord John Russell, the Home Secretary, and throughout its passage it was twinned with the Civil Marriage Bill. All the Committee Stages and Readings of the Registration Bill were followed by the equivalent stage of the Marriage Bill, thus emphasising their inter-relation. According to Lord Russell (Cobbett's *Parliamentary History*, vol. xiv, col. 368) 'a Bill to be sufficient and satisfactory for the regulation of Dissenters' marriages should be preceded by a Bill of registration'. Registration of births, deaths and marriages was 'important for the security of property—important to ascertain the state and condition of individuals under various circumstances—important to enable the Government to acquire a general knowledge of the state of the population of the country'.

Manchester refers to civil marriage as 'democratic capitalist marriage' (1980, p. 366) and Anderson calls it an 'essential facet of modernisation' (1975, p. 50) but neither spells out what I suggest is the real link between the two. Pressure had been building up for over twenty years to allow dissenters their own marriage forms. Because these would take place outside Anglican churches, and therefore had no machinery for recording them, a separate system was necessary in any event. In the meantime, the formation of the modern state machine, manned by 'Code-Napoleon-minded social engineers and statisticians' (Anderson, 1975, p. 64) made clear the need for a comprehensive system of registration. The advantages of combining the two measures were political as well as administrative. Supporters of one were more likely to submit to the other if satisfied that the two were inter-dependent. A few saw through this, apparently from the right-wing of the Anglican Church, and said that separate registers could be kept. They saw the integrated system as a means of increasing secular control over the Church 'just to gratify the statistical fancies of some philosophers' (*Hansard*, vol. xxxi, col. 378).

At a political level, then, the introduction of civil marriage was imbricated in the rapid growth of the bureaucratic state because it facilitated a registration system. Two other phenomena enrich our understanding of the political context of the Civil Marriage Act;

electoral reform and the emergence of hegemonic policies to cope with changing class relations.

The Reform Act 1832 provided a uniform borough franchise and extended the vote to the middle class. Agitation for electoral reform had threatened, at one stage, to bring down the whole political order. During the debates, the established Anglican Church was identified by radicals as part of the system of Old Corruption. Established religion, according to Johnson *et al.*, 'based on the hegemony of gentry paternalism and the rule of agrarian capital, was an integral part of the whole conservative Anglican repertoire of class-cultural relations of the eighteenth century' (Johnson, 1976, p. 24). It has even been suggested that at a critical point the disestablishment of the Church looked possible. The Church had become synonymous in the minds of the public with Toryism and indolence. It contrasted poorly with the fervour with which methodists were championing the right of the poor to have the Gospel preached to them. Church rates raised to pay absentee parsons fanned the unpopularity (Haw, 1952, p. 155).

Electoral reform brought middle class industrialists into Parliament, some of whom were either dissenters themselves or at least sympathetic to religious tolerance. Politicians of all complexions were aware that wounds had to be healed if the polity was to survive and the issue of dissenters' marriages was divisive out of all proportion to its importance to the State. Lord John Russell made several references in the parliamentary debates to the need for reconciliation. During the first reading of the Bill, he even digressed to express sympathy with nonconformist complaints about the Church rate system and the exclusion of protestant dissenters from the Universities of Oxford and Cambridge (*Hansard*, vol. xxxi, col. 378). Civil marriage can therefore be seen as an astute concession to the newly enfranchised middle class. But it was not only a concession to them. It was also directed at those sections of the working class who were clinging to traditional marriage practices.

In the previous chapter I looked briefly at the concept of hegemony in the context of a dominant class attempting to erode social practices belonging to an earlier mode of production, to impose their way of seeing the world. The problem for the *urban* gentry of the 1830s and 1840s was of a different nature. The period was one of profound dislocation at all levels—economic, political and social—and it was by no means evident that the consent of the working classes to the factory system had been won (Richards, 1980, p. 67). Most hegemonic measures prior to about 1850 were therefore concerned to promote work discipline, regularity and acceptance of the labour contract. But even at this stage there were clear attempts at wider ideological control. Primarily this was through education (Gray, 1977, p. 85) but attention was also paid to the family. The moral decay of the working class was seen in terms of deficient patterns of family life; the apparent absence of domesticity, family responsibility, thrift and accumulation. The working woman emerged as a 'social problem' in the 1830s and 1840s. Revelations about wives in paid employment 'shattered middle class complacency and aroused the reformatory zeal of Evangelical and Utilitarian philanthropists' (Alexander, 1982, p. 31). Male-dominated trades unions, for their own reasons, assisted in the propagation of the middle class family ideal. Pressure for the family wage, whereby men were to be paid an amount sufficient to support a wife and children, borrowed the bourgeois family form as its model. Whilst in reality it could not be achieved and most working class families found it impossible to rely on the man's earnings alone, the existence of the ideal clearly had effects in planting gender images into many men's minds (as well as legitimating low pay for women) (Hall, 1982, p. 26).

Storch, in an essay on middle class moral reformers in the industrial north 1825–50, discusses the fear and loathing with which the Victorian middle class viewed popular culture (Storch, 1977, p. 139). Pluralist marriage practices imported from rural homelands must have contrasted sharply with the ordered, patriarchal homelife of urban rulers. Whilst most concerted efforts to 'embourgeoise' the family took place after 1850, and I refer to these later in the chapter, it is likely that civil marriage would have been seen as a way of incorporating alternative practices into a wider net of formal marriage; particularly because the more private nature of civil marriage accorded with the desires of the middle class to celebrate their own marriages more privately anyway.

Golby and Purdue (1984, p. 85) note that the 'attempts to reform popular culture by legislation and proselytisation from above can be seen to be at one with the reform of the institutions of government and administration as society struggled to come to terms with unexpected and unplanned demographic and economic changes'. In this discussion of the political context within which civil marriage should be situated I have tried to show how state formation, electoral reform and hegemonic practices (themselves closely related phenomena) created conditions whereby civil marriage could not only be accepted but actually be seen as desirable. I now leave context and deal directly with popular reaction to Lord Hardwicke's Act and the continuation of informal marriage despite the withdrawal of legal recognition.

(b) Informal Marriage 1754–1836

The immediate effect of Lord Hardwicke's Act appears to have been a riot in Oxfordshire. The electors of that county, for the first time in forty years, went to the polls when a local Whig magnate decided to challenge the Tories' hold. The landed interest trotted out every possible slogan in order to smear the Whigs and their government (Jarrett, 1976, p. 25). In addition to emotive issues such as the 'loss' of eleven days in the previous September caused by the switch from the Julian to the Gregorian calendar and an Act of 1753 which allowed for the naturalisation of Jews, Hardwicke's Act was used to whip up a frenzy against the challenger's party. By skilfully painting a prospect of universal circumcision and a dismal future of stolen days and regulated marriages, the Tories seem to have engineered a riot amongst local freeborn Englishmen. So much of politics at this time was private—hidden from the masses—that the rare introduction of an issue for public debate was likely to lead to an over-reaction (Clark, 1982, p. 12). On the other hand, one can at least say that the Act was a measure which was capable of engendering strong feelings amongst ordinary people.

The Act was interpreted strictly by the courts. Any misdescription of the parties might invalidate the marriage. For example, in Pouget v. Tomkins (1812 2 Hag. Con. 142) the omission of one christian name invalidated the publication of the banns and was therefore fatal to the marriage. The Act struck hard at the Fleet chaplains and 'practically drove them out of business except in the bogs of Ireland' (Arnold, 1950, p. 488). One obstinate clergyman called Wilkinson purported to remove his business from the Fleet to the Savoy claiming that, by virtue of an ancient privilege, the area was extra-parochial. He is said to have celebrated 1400 clandestine marriages there after the Act came into force (Burns, 1845). Eventually the Government heard about this when one of David Garrick's company was married by Savoy licence and Garrick passed the licence to the authorities. This could be regarded as a particularly dirty trick bearing in mind that Garrick later enjoyed huge success with his play *The Clandestine Marriage*. Wilkinson's translation from the Fleet to the Savoy resulted in conviction and transportation further afield, to the American colonies (Lecky, 1883, vol. ɪ, p. 498).

Whilst the 1753 Act may have put an end to business in the Fleet, it is not entirely correct to suppose, as some historians have done, that 'the Act achieved its objective' (Manchester, 1980, p. 364) or that 'clandestine marriages were effectively eliminated' (Worsley-Boden, 1932, p. 118). It is true that the first few years of the Act would have been seen as a success by its promoters. London returns for 1760 showed a steep rise in marriages both by banns and licence (Gillis, 1980, p. 6). Licences in particular increased in popularity amongst the working classes who were now more able to afford them. By the time civil marriage was introduced in 1836 they accounted for about one third of all recorded marriages (Outhwaite, 1973, p. 62). On the other hand, recent evidence suggests that a considerable number of people declined to avail themselves of the statutory procedure. For ease of discussion, I divide them into those who engaged in evasive practices, where the authority of Hardwicke's Act was not questioned but steps were taken to evade its grip, and alternative practices, where even the right of the law to regulate marriage in this way was denied.

I say there is considerable evidence of these popular substitutes for official marriage but a few qualifications might be appropriate. Almost by definition, alternative marriage practices are not recorded in parish registers and Census schedules. Although some work has been done on evasive practices, in particular Gretna Green marriages, very little has been done on alternative ones. J.R. Gillis's writings (1980 and 1985) seem to be the only directly relevant studies and even these rely heavily on published histories of folklore (particularly Welsh folklore). Gillis seems more concerned with inter-generational conflict and the socio-psychological aspects of marriage rites. He is less persuasive in tracing a broader history of the State's regulation of marriage. Nevertheless much of what follows borrows heavily from the material he has uncovered.

Although there is no way of measuring accurately the extent to which informal (and now non-legal) marriages continued after Hardwicke's Act, a number of social historians have been impressed by the fact that they did. Scott and Tilly note that 'free unions' appear to increase after 1750, particularly amongst the emergent working class in the new towns (1975, p. 97). Stone suggests that 'up to a third of all marriages between 1753 and 1836 were illegal and void', although she cites no source (Stone, 1977, p. 31). Newman, in her study of the east

Kent parish of Ash-Next-Sandwich, speculates that 'a proportion of up to 15 per cent for non-church unions might be reasonable at this time' because 'common law marriage was a deep-rooted tradition amongst a section of the population' (Newman, 1980, p. 151).

One source of information which can be interpreted as supporting the proposition that alternative marriage practices persisted is illegitimacy statistics. I referred in chapter 2 to the way that pre-1753 illegitimacy statistics have had to be re-evaluated following the realisation that informal marriage was widespread so that the children of those unions would have been regarded as socially legitimate. Much the same re-evaluation is necessary for the period 1750 to 1850 when there was an undoubted rise in the rate of registered illegitimate births. It is now being realised that a substantial section of the registered illegitimate births after 1754 may have been to stable families who, prior to the Act, would have been accepted as validly married. Whether we can go as far as Meteyard to argue that 'the rise in recorded illegitimacy after 1753 can be ascribed in large part to the effects of Lord Hardwicke's Act' is not clear (Meteyard, 1980, p. 488). We simply do not have the data. One can agree, however, that a surge in registered illegitimacy from 1754 is consistent with the continuation of earlier marriage practices where the children could no longer be registered as legitimate.

(i)   Evasive Practices

The best known evasive tactic was the so-called Gretna Green marriage. Because the 1753 Act applied only to England and Wales, the practice developed of crossing the border and marrying according to old common law forms under which the evidenced exchange of consents was the only requirement. The dominant image of these marriages now is probably that of well-heeled lovers eloping because of parental disapproval. The classic example of that is the elopement in 1772 of a future Lord Chancellor, Lord Eldon, and Bessy Surtees, using ladder and all. In fact, many less exalted inhabitants of the border counties shared the dissenting view that marriage was a civil contract and resented being told to marry in church. This, combined with a regionally specific dislike of the Established Church anyway, meant that large sections of the population in Northumberland and Cumberland crossed the border and married under Scots law after the 1753 Act came into effect. Olive Anderson suggests that 'when the Newcastle and Carlisle, and then the Caledonian railway lines were opened, the practice became almost universal among working people' (Anderson, 1975, p. 68). Certainly, large marriage businesses developed to accommodate the trade at places like Coldstream and Lamberton Toll as well as Gretna Green. Package tours were available providing a sort of bed and breakfast service with accommodation both for celebration and consummation. Gretna Green marriages continued until 1856 when Lord Brougham's Act introduced a three-week residence qualification in Scotland. Thereafter, only wealthy elopers could afford that sort of time off. In any event, the facility of civil marriage after 1836 had already cut deeply into the trade, as we will see later in the chapter.

Border marriages were impractical to many ordinary people who lived further south. Those who wished to operate roughly within the law adopted other evasive tactics to maintain the privacy of their wedding arrangements. The most common way was to fake residence in another parish and have the banns read or the licence obtained there. This was easier for those who lived near large towns. In Exeter the practice was to come to town on three consecutive Saturday nights and 'establish' residence there by sleeping in lodgings (Gillis, 1980, p. 6). It is likely that in many towns the identity of parishioners would not have been known to the church and a simple false claim that there had been sufficient residence would not have been investigated. Draconian though it was, Lord Hardwicke's Act offered some protection to these marriages because s. 10 excluded evidence in litigation which was intended to show that the residence requirement had not been satisfied.

(ii) Alternative Practices
The apparent ubiquity of evasive practices probably meant that *alternative* marriage forms were restricted to three overlapping constituencies: those who lived in rural areas where access to the towns (and anonymity) was difficult; new arrivals in the manufacturing towns and villages who tended to bring with them old marriage forms (such as fixed-term marriage, separate property for women, built-in divorce) and those who had conscientious objections to any religious form of marriage ceremony or specifically to the Anglican one. Although these groups are not mutually exclusive they serve as convenient categories around which to order the historical evidence. One common element between them is the changed nature of the legitimacy underpinning them. Whereas the vagueness of the common law allowed participants and communities to believe that there was some legal basis underlying their marriage traditions (even if they

were wrong) it now became much more difficult to maintain this as knowledge of Hardwicke's Act spread. The new practices depended increasingly on the Court of public opinion to endow their relationship with propriety.

In rural societies it is likely that the more remote and closed they were then the more resistant they would be to legal edicts coming out of London because their internal normative order would be closely related to prevailing economic and social circumstances; even more so if they were remote even from the parson. Whereas the parson may previously have performed a mediating function in the event of conflict over marriage, perhaps by witnessing the exchange of consents, or entering an informal marriage on the register, the harsh penalties in Lord Hardwicke's Act now deterred them. Officiating over a ceremony in the knowledge that the proper requirements had not been satisfied carried the penalty of fourteen years' transportation. Whilst one parson could resent the transportation clause as 'a punishment little inferior to ye gallows and inflicted generally on the most profligate and abandoned part of mankind' (Cox, 1910, p. 92) very few of his colleagues actually risked it. Informal marriages now take on a more secular flavour with priests becoming constables of morality rather than notaries of the people's marriage business.

Wales seems to have been particularly resistant to the new law, given that the Scottish border was inaccessible, and one can link this with centuries-old practices of secular and trial marriage. The Welsh social historian Alwyn Rees noted that unformalised cohabitation in Wales survived beyond the eighteenth century and he attributed this to the tradition of 'opportunities for separation allowed under medieval Welsh law' (Rees, 1975, p. 128). The Welsh folklorist T. Gwynn Jones, writing in 1930, notes some examples of jumping the broom in 1837 and the use of the expression '*priodas fach*' (little wedding) to imply an irregular marriage contracted privately. We are also told that lifelong unformalised unions were known in many districts and Rhys suggests that one reason behind these was the retention of the woman's separate identity and surname (Rhys, 1901, p. 76).

Of particular interest is the expression '*byw tali*' which is still used in north Wales today to refer to illicit unions. T. Gwyn Jones noted that unlegalised unions were referred to as *byw tali* in Denbighshire during the nineteenth century but was unable to explain the origin. '*Byw*' is Welsh for 'living' and it is probable that 'tally' would have had a new meaning by the nineteenth century to refer to the tin tag which a miner attached to his coal tub to identify the coal as his own. Figuratively, those living together outside formal marriage wore each other's tally as a sign of temporary ownership (Notes and Queries, 13th series, i, p. 169). In Robert Roberts' account of working class life in Salford at the turn of this century he refers to the fact that those who dwelt together unmarried—livin' tally—strangely came in for little criticism despite the otherwise strict sexual code that prevailed (Roberts, 1973, p. 46). Gwenith Gwyn, whilst looking through the baptism registers of the parish of Ceiriog Valley for the period 1768–1805, discovered that a staggering 60 per cent of all births were attributed to conjugal arrangements which were not solemnised in church (and were therefore non-legal). They had been kept by the vicar in a separate category from the few 'illegitimate births' where no father was declared (Gwyn, 1928, pp. 153–4). This was presumably the nearest a priest dared go to recognising officially marriage forms which now had no legal effect. One simply has no idea how many other parts of Wales retained earlier marriage forms to such a degree.

Nor do we really know how long they continued. One recent study of the folklore of the Welsh border has discovered the practice of wife-selling as late as 1882 (Simpson, 1976, pp. 118–19). In that year a woman maintained in the County Court at Chester that she was not living in adultery because her first husband had 'legally' sold her for 25 shillings and she had a stamped receipt to prove it. Given that wife-selling was an informal institution of a similar nature to formless marriage one can speculate that State approved marriage entry did not take hold until well into the nineteenth century.

There is one argument why there might actually have been a renaissance in pluralist marriage customs in the late eighteenth century. Successive agricultural crises in the latter part of the century, coupled with the vagrancy produced by enclosure of common land, increased reliance on the Poor Law. The basis of poor relief was 'settlement', or attachment to a particular parish. On legal marriage, the woman's right of settlement ceased and the husband's parish became liable. If the husband deserted, the wife's original parish would disclaim responsibility and the husband's own parish often attempted to do the same (the husband being unavailable to assert the validity of the marriage). It was safer, therefore, for a woman to engage in a little wedding which was recognised by those of her class as a proper marriage but which preserved her original right of settlement should anything go wrong (Anderson, 1975, p. 52). When the Royal Commissioners on the Poor Law discovered the apparent practice of mothers deliberately remaining 'unmarried' this is what they may have been witnessing.

Many rural traditions were brought into urban areas. Intercourse retained its rural significance as a commitment. Although betrothal had ceased to have legal force after 1753, women relied on communal pressure to support them so that should they become pregnant the man would be forced to go through a marriage ceremony. There was also the threat, prior to the bastardy clauses in the Poor Law Amendment Act 1834, that paternity would be sworn against the man. Should this fail, there was still little shame attached to pre-marital pregnancy and they could fall back on their own labour or family (Gillis, 1985, pp. 127 and 180–2). As urbanisation continued, however, marriage beliefs moved away from being custom and family based and were organised more on class and gender lines. Life in the early industrial towns differed in two respects from rural life-styles. First, workers were much more mobile, moving from one part of the town to another and from town to town. Second, the sexual division of labour was less marked than in rural areas. The combined effect of these was that, in addition to rural practices being imported to the towns, new ones also developed.

The social investigator Patrick Colquhoun noted at the turn of the nineteenth century 'the prodigious number among the lower classes who cohabit together without marriage' (cited in Thompson, 1968, p. 60). Half a century later the chronicler of the London Poor, Henry Mayhew, observed that with costermongers 'concubinage among persons of all ages was the rule and marriage the exception' (Mayhew, 1861, p. 459). At the end of the century Charles Booth in his *Life and Labour of the London Poor* wrote that 'with the lowest classes premarital relations are very common, perhaps even usual . . . I believe it to constitute one of the clearest lines of demarcation between upper and lower in the working class' (Booth, 1902–3, 3rd series, vol. ɪ, pp. 55–6). Common to all three writers, although less so with Mayhew, was a tendency to attribute this to immorality and promiscuity rather than to a particular form of temporary marriage. If one views these practices from the perspective of the participants, much of the information we have takes on a quite different light.

The trades to which these people belonged were highly mobile ones. Street vendors were constantly changing their patch, soldiers and sailors were liable to be stationed or based elsewhere, canal and railway navvies, apprentices, servants and miners had to move to where the work was. Practices of exchanging rings and of little weddings evinced a desire for public recognition of a temporary status so that intercourse was regarded as respectable and children legitimate. Returning the ring in urban areas seems to have fulfilled the same function as jumping backwards over the broom in the country (Coleman, 1965, pp. 32 and 181–96). Lewis Morris describes the little wedding, or *priodas fach*, of the South Wales valleys in the 1760s (Ifan, 1972, p. 201):

> Some couples (especially among the miners) either having no friends, or seeing this kind of public marriage too troublesome or impracticable, procure a man to wed them privately which will not cost above two or three mugs of ale. Sometimes half a dozen couples agree to a merry meeting, and are thus wedded and bedded together. This they call priodas fach and is frequently made use of among miners and others to make sure of a woman . . . The little wedding doth not bind them so effectually but that after a month's trial they may part by consent, when the miner leaves his mistress, and removes to a minework in some distant country, and the girl is not worse looked upon by the miners than if she had been an unspotted virgin.

The respectability of the union depended, therefore, on the public legitimation of the arrangement. It is for this reason that Mayhew was able to say that 'chance children' (that is, where the father was unknown) were extremely rare among the women of costermongers and that the informally married costers were 'as faithful to each other as an English properly married couple would be' (Mayhew, 1861, pp. 20–1).

The unprecedented mobility of a substantial section of the English and Welsh labour force can only partially explain the survival and adaptation of old marriage forms, however. Changing gender relations are equally important. In some areas at some times the economic power of women increased, through access to wage labour as costers, dust-collectors and chimney sweeps, and one possible use of it was to *refuse* marriage rather than insist upon it. Gillis notes that in Culcheth, south Lancashire, the rise of illegitimacy coincided precisely with the growth of cotton weaving (Gillis, 1985, pp. 207–8) and this encouraged women to seek more equal relationships. The breakdown of the guild system meant that many men could no longer hope to become self-employed in their own craft and a union with an income-producing woman was essential to survival. This in turn allowed women to name their price, which was often cohabitation rather than marriage.

Economic independence could be gained through self-employment as well as wage-labour. Early urbanisation offered opportunities for women to build up capital and income by opening an inn or conducting a trade. Legal marriage, involving as it did the transfer of ownership and control of property to the husband, was highly unattractive to some of them. It presumably also confused their creditors which may partly explain an announcement placed in a newspaper by a self-employed London chimney-sweep, Mary Vinson, in 1787 (Pinchbeck, 1930, p. 285):

> Many in the same business have reported that I am married again, which is totally false and without foundation, it being calculated to mislead my customers.

The implication of this is that a woman's reputation of creditworthiness could be lost at a stroke if she married legally, because creditors and customers would not know how reliable the husband was. She was safer, therefore, exchanging rings before witnesses which gave popular sanction to the relationship without the legal consequences.

In addition one must remember the point made above that retaining settlement with her own parish might be better insurance for a woman than a formal marriage certificate. The Irish in large towns and ports could usually find a catholic priest to marry them illegally. The Royal Commission on the Poor Law seems to have understood this. According to the Report (1834, p. 99):

> These marriages satisfy the conscience of the wife, and while no relief is required of the parish, their invalidity is unknown or unattended to. But as soon as the man becomes chargeable and the parish proceeds to remove him and his family, he shows that he is not legally married, and his children claim settlement on the parishes in which they were born.

Family strategy, then, was interwoven with the prevailing forms of social security, in a curious parallel with the operation of the cohabitation rule today.

Whilst many women used unofficial marriage forms, some of those who did not still tried to invoke popular customs to mitigate the discriminatory aspects of formal marriage. In chapter 2 I described the smock wedding which, it was believed, allowed a woman who married wearing only her smock to retain separate legal identity.

These continued throughout the period 1753 to 1836. Gillis (1985, p. 151) refers to attempts during the marriage ceremony itself to qualify the terms of the contract. In Yorkshire, for example, the clergy found it difficult to keep control of proceedings. The women endeavoured to keep a thumb free when the hands were clasped as a sign that they meant not to be dominated. By the end of this period, legal marriage was becoming essential for most working class girls as they were gradually squeezed out of the labour force. Male workers exerted material pressure whilst the campaigns of middle class reformers combined with the widely-sung horrors of factory life (Branca, 1978, p. 46) exerted ideological pressure. Furthermore, the Poor Law Amendment Act 1834 must have made legal marriage much more attractive. In a kind of pincer movement it removed both public and private rights by taking away outdoor relief and affiliation proceedings from unmarried mothers. As a result of these factors, many working class girls could scarcely survive unmarried and most of them had married by their mid-twenties (Weeks, 1981, p. 68).

The third constituency which engaged in alternative, non-legal, marriage could broadly be called dissent. Many people believed that marriage was a purely secular contract and thus objected to the notion of going through any form of religious ceremony. The popular practice of crossing the border after Hardwicke's Act is witness to this. It did not necessarily connote atheism, merely a particular position on marriage, although some non-border areas such as Woking in Surrey which had a tradition of religious dissent became detached from all religion after the Act and turned to militant secularism (Bickley, 1902, pp. 25–9).

Little work seems to have been done on the attitude of nonconformist groups towards the law in the early nineteenth century. The returns to Parliament in 1811 indicated only 2655 Anglican churches compared with 3 451 dissenting chapels (Bennett, 1839, p. 261) and one speculates that a large proportion of these conducted their own marriage services. It can certainly be inferred from what was said during the Parliamentary debates over the Civil Marriage Bill that avoidance was widespread. Lord John Russell, when introducing the Bill, acknowledged that marriage registration could not be effective whilst marriage was restricted to the established Church and conceded that dissenting marriages were sufficiently prevalent to distort seriously the official statistics (*Hansard*, vol. xxxi, col. 369 and 373). It is unnecessary to say any more about the religious basis for ignoring Lord Hardwicke's Act. It flowed from a generalised hostility to the Anglican Church: a hostility which parliamentarians by the 1830s knew would not go away and had to be diffused.

(c) The Passage of the Act

The debates over the 1836 Bill are far less revealing than those over Lord Hardwicke's Bill, although some of the *absences* are significant. Gone is the strident confidence with which law-makers imposed their own marriage forms on an unwilling populace. Instead we hear the soothing tones of Lord John Russell who (*Hansard*, vol. xxxi, col. 373):

> could not help feeling [the 1753 Act] was unjust and was an unnecessary violation of the consciences of those who dissented from the Church.

Gone is the panic over the seduction of young heirs and heiresses and the danger to property from this form of social mobility. Instead we hear the limp objection that the civil ceremony would 'allow the son of any gentleman in England to marry the housemaid' (Mr Arthur Trevor, MP) which receives the brisk retort from a leading dissenter 'if the son of a gentleman chose to marry the housemaid, he is quite at liberty to do so in the Church as any other place' (Mr Baines, MP, *Hansard*, vol. xxxiv, col. 1036).

Gone too is the neurosis over clandestinity. Instead Parliament permits, as we will see, marriage by licence after seven days notice in a Notice Book, which is hardly a blaze of publicity. Further it was explicitly recognised by the eminent family lawyer, Dr. Lushington, 'that it is impossible, by the agency of Banns, to prevent clandestine marriages' (*Hansard* vol. xxxiv, col. 132). In fact, the only opposition to the marriage provisions (as opposed to the details of the registration system) is the grotesque suggestion that requiring the Board of Guardians to sit through the reading of all Marriage Notices might overwork the poor wee things (Mr Wilks, MP, *Hansard*, vol. xxxv, col. 1123).

How should one view this marked difference in tone between the two sets of debates? The most obvious point is that marriage had ceased to be the linchpin in the circulation of property. Whereas in the mid-eighteenth century the primary form of wealth was still land, a century later over 50 per cent of the national capital was in durable assets other than land. Marriage and primogeniture, in a sense, were

less central to the political and economic system and so parental
control was less of an issue. Apart from a rather obscure section
(s. 43) which provides that in cases of fraudulent marriage the
Attorney-General could sue for the forfeiture of property accruing
from the fraud (a section which appears not to have been litigated
upon) the new marriage code is unconcerned with the disruption of
property through improvident marriages. Another factor in the
altered tone may have been the admission into politics of the middle
class by the 1832 Reform Act which introduced greater heterogeneity
of views into the legislative process. The impression of unity of
interest, despite disagreement over detail, which characterised the
1753 debates is gone in 1835. Throughout, the Home Secretary, Lord
John Russell, has to be the embodiment of conciliation and liber-
alism.

Although the provisions of the Act are as dry as old bones, and I
will omit much of the detail, there are two reasons why a survey of
the major provisions is necessary. First, it underlines the extent to
which the rigid draconian measures in Lord Hardwicke's Act had
been departed from. Second, some of the detailed links between this
Act and the contemporaneous Acts to amend the Poor Law and to
institute a registration system must be traced.

The proposals in the Marriage Bill were not entirely unknown to
English law. During the Commonwealth, marriages had been taken
out of the hands of the clergy and given to justices of the peace (see
the Civil Marriage Act 1653 and Hill, 1975, p. 136). Nevertheless, the
framework of regular marriage formation remained within the parish
system, relying as it did on the publication of banns, and the Act
lapsed on the Restoration. The 1836 Act was more innovatory and
provided a diversity of choice almost unique in nineteenth-century
Europe, although similar measures were introduced in some other
common law jurisdictions (Wood, 1975, p. 255 and Duncan, 1978, p.
215). In the words of one religious historian, it was 'nothing short of a
revolution in the forms and ceremonies of marriage' (Arnold, 1950,
p. 491).

Basically, the Act added five new forms of marriage entry to the
two existing ones (of marriage by banns and by licence). Now one
could marry within the Church of England on production of the
Superintendent Registrar's Certificate. One could also marry in a
registered building (such as some dissenting places of worship) with
or without a civil licence (depending on the fee paid and the period of
residence and notice given) and one could marry in a register office

with or without civil licence. The requirement of notice was common to the new forms and notice could only be given to the Superintendent Registrar of the district in which the parties had resided for at least seven days. If the parties had lived in separate districts then notice had to be given to each Superintendent Registrar. Some attempt was made, therefore, to establish a local connection but this must have been for statistical requirements of the State because the publicity was feeble; notices were entered in a book which was open for public inspection. It was possible for anyone, presumably a parent, to enter 'forbidden' against a name and there was provision for the entry of a general caveat against the granting of certificates or licences to a specified person. This would prevent the wedding until the caveat was cleared away.

During the currency of the notice period, the Notice had to be read to meetings of the Board of Guardians of that Poor Law District. Section 6 assumes that the Superintendent Registrar is also the Clerk to the Board of Guardians but provides that if he is not then he must transmit the Notices to the appropriate Clerk. The intention here must have been to give the Guardians sufficient time to lean on would-be spouses and deter so-called improvident marriages. Presumably they acted from a position of strength because of their discretion whether to grant outdoor relief or workhouse employment; the former obviously being preferable, if only because the spouses would be separated in the latter. If, on the other hand, the woman was already pregnant, the lever of the Poor Law could be used to force through a marriage. Gillis tells us of one register office wedding in the 1840s when George Stiffell was pressured into marrying Ellen Barrett. When Stiffell baulked at the idea of a marriage without a ring, the Guardians offered to pay for it (Gillis, 1980, p. 16).

The Act laid down procedures for the registration of nonconformist places of worship and certain minimum requirements about the ceremony itself. The alternative to a nonconformist ceremony was a register office wedding. It is interesting that the tone of the Act implies that these would be few. Section 21, which authorises these weddings, is prefaced with the words 'And be it enacted that any Persons who shall object to marry under the provisions of this Act in any such registered Building . . .' thus giving the impression that the purely secular ceremony was intended for a fractious minority. Lord John Russell's view, when introducing the Bill that 'the class of persons' using this procedure 'certainly was not very numerous' confirms this (*Hansard*, vol. XXXI, col. 377).

The emphasis in virtually every section of the Act is on collation of data, issue of licences, return of registers to London and the extent of jurisdiction; all of which one would expect a State in the process of modernisation to require. All conceivable eventualities are governed by the Act: the type of Marriage Notice Book to be kept; the forms of Certificates and Licences to be issued (and the different watermarks to be printed on the paper); the method of appointing registrars and Superintendent Registrars; the procedures for registering Chapels (and what happens if the congregation wants to move to a new building); the information which must be sent periodically to London, and so on. A study of the system erected by the Marriage and Registration Acts would probably disclose the ideal type of Weber's concept of bureaucracy. To emphasise the integration of the new marriage law with the general system of registration being set up, it is provided (probably unnecessarily) in s. 44 that 'this Act shall be taken to be part of the said Act for registering Births, Deaths and Marriages, as fully and effectually as if incorporated therewith . . .'. The point of underlining all this is to stress what I said earlier: legislation on dissenters' marriages might well not have been introduced without the State being convinced that it would facilitate the much-needed registration system. The fact that earlier attempts to give relief to dissenters had failed (in 1824, 1825, 1834 and 1835) strengthens the argument that the grievance on its own was not sufficiently compelling.

3.   INFORMAL MARRIAGE 1836–1927

This section takes us to the end of a distinctive period in the evolution of English marriage law. We have now dealt with the two major pieces of legislation which replaced customary practices responsive to local conditions with precise marriage codes uniformly applied. By the mid-nineteenth century an age of conformity had begun which only began to fragment with the increase in cohabitation after the Second World War. For many working class people in about 1850 alternatives to formal marriage were becoming decreasingly attractive. The amendment to the Poor Law in 1834 made legal marriage increasingly important for women's economic survival. Towns and cities became more anonymous so that there was less effective community pressure on a man to marry or support a woman if she had a child by him. The bourgeois family model slowly filtered down to the working class so that alternative forms became less thinkable. But above all industrial capitalism undermined the independence of the family economy producing sharper gender stratification; men were principal breadwinners, women were dependent wives and mothers (Gillis, 1985, p. 241).

As we will see, unmarried cohabitation in the cities, particularly London, was common for much of the nineteenth century but, in the typology I use for this book, it was more cohabitation than informal marriage. It tended to lose the symbolism of exchanging rings before witnesses or ritually presenting the key to the door. Although a far from perfect analogy, it became more like what we imagine student cohabitation to be today: an intimate relationship more conveniently carried on under the same roof but underpinned by uncertainties about the future. I should stress that this was only a tendency and many nineteenth-century unions produced children. The movement generally, however, was towards the production of children within formal marriage so that informal relationships fell into more specific, although overlapping, categories. First, there were the urban young I have mentioned above. Second, and in contrast with the modern perception of cohabitation, informal unions were not uncommon amongst older people; one obvious explanation being that they were hanging on to earlier cultural forms. Barton has analysed a large number of reported cases between 1679 and 1938 where the issue was whether a contract was void by reason of sexual immorality. Although the courts tended to emphasise the sexual aspects of the relationship, dismissing some as being comparable with prostitution, the facts of the cases often revealed informal marriages of long duration and stability—in one case over thirty years (Barton, 1985, p. 38). One infers that many of the parties were upper working class and middle class because there must have been sufficient property at stake to make litigation worthwhile.

Third, there was cohabitation brought about through the absence of legal divorce. Although I have mentioned divorce at various stages in the context of informal practices building in their own forms of divorce, it is probable that the absence of legal divorce (from all but a tiny minority) only became really significant as a factor in cohabitation in the mid-nineteenth century. If marriage behaviour takes place within a normative order dislocated from the general law then the disabilities of that general law are less likely to affect the minds of participants. Furthermore, after 1753 informal marriages had no legal effect so that no legal divorce was necessary and bigamy was not committed if one party then engaged in a formal marriage. Prior to an effective registration system, it is probable that someone formally married could engage with impunity in a further bigamous marriage in a different district. After a registration system was set up and *seen* to be set up, however, the risks of detection were presumably perceived to be higher. Whilst it now appears that bigamy trials tended only to follow when the original spouse made trouble, and there is a suggestion that sentences were quite lenient (Colwell, 1980, p. 91), one assumes that this was not widely known at the time.

Although the period 1837–1927 can generally be categorised as a movement towards uniformity, it is not without interest from the point of view of this study. I look first at informal marriage and cohabitation to develop the discussion of the dialectical relationship between family behaviour and marriage law. I then deal with two legal episodes which throw light on how the law adopts assimilative and deterrent strategies to control family formation.

(a) Family Formation after the Marriage Act 1836

The major research on popular acceptance of civil marriage in the mid-nineteenth century has been carried out by Olive Anderson (1975). Making good use of the fact that between 1837 and 1884 the Registrar-General's obligatory annual report to Parliament had to contain abstracts of marriages in each of the 620 districts (and not just each registration county and division), she provides a fascinating picture of the differential take-up rate throughout England and Wales. She takes civil marriage to mean register office marriage so that marriage in a registered noncomformist chapel is counted, in her typology, as a religious ceremony.

Prior to 1856, register office weddings were not particularly popular if one looks at the national statistics. In 1844, about 3 per cent of all marriages in England and Wales took place in a register office (Registrar-General's 7th Annual Report, 1844, p. 160). This appears to have been a result of the association between civil marriage and the Poor Law. In its first phase, civil marriage was regarded as a lower caste mode of alliance and it seems that many alternative and evasive practices continued. We know from a number of sources that people continued to cross into Scotland to be married in the border towns even though the secular nature of these ceremonies differed little in substance from the exchange of promises which took place in a register office. Similarly, the practice continued of establishing residence in a nearby large town for the sole purpose of contracting a private church marriage. I mentioned earlier that Exeter was a good example of such a town and it is interesting that John Fowles' perceptive novel about Victorian morality *The French Lieutenant's Woman* uses Exeter as the refuge for the heroine fleeing from the social conventions of Lyme Regis. Fowles describes it as 'notoriously a place to hide' and filled with 'a whole population in retreat from the claustrophobic villages and small towns of Devon' (1969, p. 65).

Register office marriages received a major boost as a result of legislation in 1856 which substituted the simple posting up of marriage notices in the Superintendent-Registrar's office for the inquisition before Poor Law Guardians. It also required three weeks' residence in Scotland before a valid marriage could be contracted there. As Anderson says, 'after 1856 civil marriage provided all over the country that widely desired but hitherto unobtainable combination: a way of marriage that was both cheap (fees totalling only seven shillings) and entirely free from publicity (1975, p. 65). It is at this stage that the assimilative legislation begins to bite by making inroads into the alternative marriage practices which had continued despite Lord Hardwicke's Act 1753. Although the national rate of register office marriage in 1864 had risen to only 8 per cent, there were now marked regional variations. The three areas where secular marriage was most popular were the northern border counties, Wales and Monmouthshire and Devon and Cornwall. In the peak period of the 1860s and 1870s, between 40 per cent and 65 per cent of all marriages in these regions were register office marriages (to which should be added 10 per cent for marriage in noncomformist chapels) (Registrar-General's 27th Annual Report, 1864, pp. ix and 4).

Anderson claims that the frequency of civil marriage in these regions reflects either 'the survival of very old traditions and habits or the adoption of new ways of behaviour under the shock of economic transformation' (1975, p. 86). This claim has led to a debate amongst social historians. Floud and Thane argue that the complications surrounding nonconformist chapel weddings (a civil registrar had to be present at the ceremony) led to many dissenters choosing the secular alternative (1979, p. 146). Furthermore, they suggest (with some justification) that an explanation which comprises both survival of the old and shock of the new is conveniently all-embracing. Anderson's rejoinder disputes Floud and Thane's interpretation of chapel marriage statistics and suggests that if there was any flaw in her original argument it was that too little attention had been paid to the social cultures of those areas where register office marriage was highest. This last point harmonises with some of the material presented here. I have argued that informal marriage tended to be regionally specific in the mid-eighteenth century. In the border counties of northern England, the secular exchange of promises whilst holding hands (handfasting) is widely recorded. In Wales, the custom of jumping the broom was prevalent. And in the southern counties of England, the idea of marriage only taking place when the bride was pregnant is well-known. One can speculate that the enthusiasm with which civil marriage was greeted in some of these regions is evidence of a continuity with traditional marriage forms. In other words, civil marriage was the successor to informal marriage.

Whilst civil marriage could not provide in-built divorce, popular practices of 'respectable' separation continued to meet this need. It is possible that emigration became regarded as morally dissolving a marriage in addition to the more formal practices of 'wife-selling' and jumping back over the broom. In Hardy's *Jude the Obscure*, Arabella emigrates to Australia because of the failure of her marriage to Jude. She re-marries in Sydney and, on her return, tells Jude that she regards that marriage as the real one. Linguistic evidence may support the proposition that civil marriage served essentially the same constituency as informal marriage, as register office weddings were popularly known as 'broomstick weddings' long after the practice of jumping the broom had died out (Bloom, 1929, and Gillis, 1980, p. 17).

With the Marriage Act 1836, the law recovered much of the ground it had lost in 1753 when it turned its back on the people's marriage forms but the wheel did not come full circle. Many historians have remarked on the prevalence of 'illicit unions' in Victorian times. Chesney suggests that in the 'borders of the underworld', 'only about one couple in ten, it seems, were legally wedded'. No honour attached to the married state and no shame to concubinage (Chesney, 1972, p. 13). He notes in a glossary of cockney vocabulary that there was an accepted expression for this arrangement, 'to dab it up'. Weeks, in a study of the regulation of sexuality since 1800 suggests that 'common law partnerships' remained popular and may even have increased in the nineteenth century (Weeks, 1981, p. 60). In rural areas too there is evidence of continued informal practices. 'Bundling', or courting in bed, survived into the mid-nineteenth century. In the 1840s the chaplain to the bishop of Bangor complained that the householders of Anglesey tacitly agreed, when hiring servants, to provide opportunities for fornication. Two decades later, the archdeacon of St Davids claimed that 'bastardy was common and unchastity the rule' among farmhouse servants in south Wales (Horn, 1980, p. 235). The old economic imperatives still held true in these areas. Where future husbands were small farmers who would require the help of children in tilling their holding, it was important for fertility to be proved before marriage took place.

But the days of widespread diversity of practice were largely over, for the time being. Urban underworlds and remote rural areas apart, the majority of people now married in register offices, churches or chapels and the law seemed to cater for majority tastes. The substance of Lord Hardwicke's Act and the Civil Marriage Act still survives today, although obviously in amended form. The age of consent was raised from twelve for a girl and fourteen a boy to sixteen for both sexes by the Age of Marriage Act 1929. Minor changes in procedure were introduced by the Marriage Act 1949. More recently, the Marriage Act 1983 has made special provision for the marriage of house-bound and detained persons and the Marriage (Prohibited Degrees of Relationship) Act 1986 has cut further into the restrictions on marriage between affines. The major assault on marriage law, in my submission, has been the growth of cohabitation law which, in a practical sense, is slowly redefining marriage in a way which has continuities with earlier legislative episodes. Two legal skirmishes in the first half of the twentieth century link the earlier and later battles.

(b) The Deceased Wife's Sister's Marriage Act 1907

(i) The History

Marriage to a deceased wife's younger sister (in other words, to a former sister-in-law) has a long tradition, particularly in the poorer classes. The high rate of death during childbirth was one particular reason why a widower might be left with infant children to look after. The practice was for an unmarried younger sister of the deceased to move into the home and look after the children. As Cretney says 'physical propinquity led to emotional involvement. What could be more natural than marriage?' (Cretney, 1984, p. 37). The legal validity of these marriages has a chequered history which is set out well in Wolfram's recent book on kinship and marriage in England (Wolfram, 1987). Briefly, biblical authority on the lawfulness of the union is ambiguous, with an apparent conflict between Leviticus and Deuteronomy (Behrman, 1968, p. 483 and Anderson, 1982, p. 67). The Christian churches had long opposed marriage between a man and his sister-in-law. The basis for the opposition was that on the original marriage the couple had become one flesh and the subsequent marriage was therefore effectively incestuous as being between the man and his own sister.

After the Reformation, the Anglican church wished to continue the proscription but had to tread carefully. Henry VIII's marital career was diverse and any tinkering with the marriage laws seemed to have some embarrassing consequence or other. Henry's first wife had been his deceased brother's wife and, although this is the reverse of the position that normally caused the trouble, the degree of proximity was the same. To insist that the marriage had been void anyway would presumably have destroyed the pretence for the split with Rome.

As a result of ambiguously worded statutes, and probably conflicting positions under common and ecclesiastical law, it was not possible to say with certainty until 1835 whether these marriages were valid. At least until 1753, this happy state of confusion neatly illustrated the general confusion over how marriage was validly to be contracted and provided the necessary room for movement to allow most people to carry on their lives without breaking any explicit law. Prior to 1835, the precise status of these unions is probably that they were voidable; in other words valid unless they were avoided before either of the parties died. If the couple were anxious about the marriage being impeached a legal ruse could be employed whereby a friend would bring a suit challenging the marriage but would fail to adduce any evidence. This effectively blocked anyone else from bringing a similar suit and the marriage was protected until the death of one of the couple, whereupon it could not be impugned.

In 1835, however, and almost out of the blue, an Act was passed making marriages with a deceased wife's sister void *ab initio* rather than merely voidable. The precise reasons behind this Act (generally known as Lord Lyndhurst's Act) are obscure. It seems that the purpose was to guarantee the legitimacy, and thus the inheritance, of the son of the seventh Duke of Beaufort; the seventh Duke having married his deceased wife's half-sister. The Act confirmed the validity of *existing* marriages but declared all future ones within the prohibited degrees totally void. The ban seems to have arisen rather suddenly in the debates and was not fully discussed. It appears that the opponents believed that the deceased wife's sister would soon be exempted from the prohibited degrees (Anderson, 1982, p. 67). So, in what was really a quarrel amongst the country's rulers, the law changed in a way which drastically affected the lives of many ordinary people. There is, therefore, a striking similarity between this Act and Lord Hardwicke's Act: both were attempts to solve a domestic problem (in all senses) by a generalised solution. And both gave rise to popular hostility.

(ii)   The Reform Campaign
After a plethora of pamphlets, countless petitions to Parliament, forty-six sessions of debate, eighteen successful second readings in the House of Commons, one Royal Commission report, annual leaders in *The Times* and the formation of two pressure groups, marriage with a deceased wife's sister was made legal in 1907. And this was only the product of a minority of the middle class. The mass of people, who were effectively excluded from the political process, appear to have carried on largely as before and simply ignored the change in the law made in 1835. As with other marriage practices, evidence is difficult to come by. *The Report of the Royal Commission appointed to Inquire into the State and Operation of the Law of Marriage as Relating to the Prohibited Degrees of Affinity and to Marriages Solemnised Abroad or in the British Colonies* (1848) gave the results of a private enquiry conducted over a three month period in five selected districts of the country. Some attempt was made to cover both urban and rural areas but the survey was by no means comprehensive. It was reported that in the eleven years since Lord Lyndhurst's Act, 1364 prohibited marriages had been contracted in the sample areas and that nearly 90 per cent of them had been contracted with a deceased wife's sister. Furthermore, as Behrman notes, 'the investigators for the survey admitted that it was very difficult to get information from the working class, so that on the whole they had confined their enquiries to the middle class' (Behrman, 1968, p. 493). The evidence that there is points, therefore, to a significant continuation of the practice despite change in its legal status.

Support for this proposition comes from a number of sources, in particular popular fiction and nineteenth-century biographies. References to the issue of 'the deceased wife's sister' (the word 'marriage' was dropped because everyone knew what was being referred to) appeared in a number of novels in the same way that clandestine marriages had exercised the minds of the literate public a century earlier. One blatantly propagandist novel entitled *The Inheritance of Evil, or the Consequences of Marrying a Deceased Wife's Sister* was published in 1849 by an anonymous writer obviously not keen on the idea (Tillotson, 1954, p. 15).

Most allusions, however, were sympathetic. E.M. Forster wrote a biography of his great-aunt, Marianne Thornton, in which he tells of the bitterness and upheaval caused in the Thornton family by the marriage in 1859 of Marianne's brother to his deceased wife's sister (Forster, 1956, chapter 6). The father of Tom Mann, the syndicalist and radical socialist, married his former sister-in-law after his first wife had died when Tom was three years old. Tom Mann's widow, Dona Torr, later wrote his biography and the footnote to the incident reads 'marriage with a "deceased wife's sister" was kept illegal by the House of Lords till 1907 despite persistent radical demands but, except where feudal tyranny in the village interfered, the law was frequently disregarded by the working class' (Torr, 1956, vol. i, p. 23). And then there was Thomas Hardy, alert as usual to the tension between family behaviour and family laws. In the closing stages of *Tess of the D'Urbervilles*, shortly before Tess is taken away to be hanged for murder, she tells Angel Clare that he must marry her younger sister, Liza-Lu. When Angel points out that 'she is my sister-in-law' Tess replies 'That's nothing dearest. People marry sister-laws continually about Marlott' (Hardy, 1960, p. 512).

In addition to references in accessible literature, it is surprising how many unpublished family documents and anecdotes of colleagues reveal similar skeletons in the cupboard. One of my former colleagues whilst researching into the history of cremation wrote to a descendant of Captain Thomas Hanham, the stoker of Woking, who was regarded as the founder of cremation in the country. Hanham married his deceased wife's sister (after an intervening marriage). Another colleague tells how his grandmother married her brother-in-law in 1902 after her sister had died. Being a middle class family they felt forced to leave the area and marry in London. The Gadsden family seemed to survive this blot on its escutcheon and provided a future Lord Mayor of London.

The issue even entered the operetta of the time. In Gilbert and Sullivan's *Iolanthe*, Strephon is sent by the Queen of the Fairies to settle the legislative question. The relevant couplet goes:

And he shall prick that annual blister,
Marriage with Deceased Wife's Sister.

This was written in 1882 and Gilbert could not have known how annual the blister was to become. As Behrman notes, after 1882 the question came up in every Parliament except two until 1907 (Behrman, 1968, p. 483). Arguments over the reform were both biblical and social. It was undoubtedly seen by some as a battle between Church and State. The Church establishment, having suffered defeat when judicial divorce was introduced by the Matrimonial Causes Act 1857, was anxious to re-assert the role of the scriptures in guiding secular legislation and to preserve its monopoly over interpretation of them. I am more concerned with the social arguments, however, and these are well summarised by Wolfram (1987, pp. 31 *et seq*.). There were three main issues; the effect on the position of a maternal aunt caring for a widower's children, the effect on the relations between sisters and the effect on the relations between a man and his sister-in-law. Space does not permit a full examination of these arguments and I pick out those aspects which are relevant to this study as a whole. In exchanges during the debates, prevailing ideologies about class, gender and sexuality came to the surface. Many conceded that for the poorer classes such a reform could be 'beneficial'. It would convert cohabitation into marriage thus ensuring 'a family' for the children (and this was also the Royal Commission's view in 1847 (1848, p. 285). This perspective should be seen as part of the wider drive to moralise the working class. Jeffrey Weeks describes such campaigns as 'attempted colonisation' and argues that the aim 'clearly was to bring the masses into accord with the perceived notions of naturalness and stability that the bourgeoisie adhered to and to which the lower middle classes aspired' (Weeks, 1981, p. 32).

But the reformers were caught in a contradiction. Apart from a nagging feeling that immorality amongst the masses should not be rewarded, the proposal to legalise such unions struck right at the heart of the bourgeois family. Lord Shaftesbury's *cri de couer* that it 'is the sanctity of home life, and the peace and purity of the English home, which are threatened by this Bill' (*Hansard*, vol. 181, col. 357) was a perceptive reference to a common domestic arrangement amongst the middle class. This was for a wife's younger sister to live in the family as nurse and housekeeper without actually being mistress of the home: the archetypal maiden aunt. There may have been a material basis for this kinship practice. Whilst there is nothing to suggest that, demographically, more bourgeois women than men were born (and wars or occupational hazards made no significant inroads into the middle class male population) the impression of the time was that there was a surplus of single women. The 1851 Census revealed that 40 per cent of women aged between 21 and 44 fell into the category of unmarried 'redundant' women. Certainly the spinster was seen as a 'family problem'. Happily (for everyone, except perhaps her) a solution was at hand. She could live in her sister's household, help with the children and free Mama (and, it should be said, Papa) for other tasks.

As a result, the opponents of reform argued that it would destroy marital morals if the sexual taboo on sisters-in-law were removed. As Harrison puts it (1979, p. 145):

> once a wife's sister could be looked on as an attractive, marriage-able person by the husband, his relationship to her and hers to him would be quite changed. Husbands would be tempted to put away their wives and seduce their sisters-in-law, who in turn would see themselves as supplanters of their sisters' beds. It would be impossible (because offensive to delicacy and purity) for maiden maternal aunts to live in their sisters' home any more.

This attitude, held by Gladstone amongst others, gives a neat insight into Victorian assumptions about sexuality; that it was an urge which could only be resisted with the help of laws, conventions and taboos. Davidoff suggests that sexuality in Victorian England, and particularly male sexuality, became the focus of a more generalised fear of disorder and of a continuing battle to tame natural forces (Davidoff, 1983, p. 20). This perhaps provides a wider context in which the controversy can be situated.

The reasons why the reform campaign was ultimately successful are complicated and to a certain extent speculative. Superficially, the Deceased Wife's Sister's Marriage Act 1907 was passed to bring the municipal law into line with that of the British colonies, described by Lord Shaftesbury as 'carrying the feeling of imperialism too far' (*Hansard*, vol. 181, col. 357). Underlying reasons may relate to attitudinal changes typical of an advanced industrial society. At a political level, the large Liberal majority in Parliament inclined to the view, ideologically, that the State should not interfere in private lives. It was the freedom of choice argument that convinced Gladstone to change his position, for example. In reality, however, the reform enabled the State to reach further into the family patterns of the working class. Jane Lewis has provided a detailed account of the reconstruction of family intervention after the Boer War and this measure might be seen as part of that process (Lewis, 1980). It may be significant that the following year saw the introduction of the crime of incest and this is another example of an official stance of *laissez-faire* masking a policy of greater legal and ideological construction and unification.

Another factor in the reform campaign's success may have been the changing nature of the middle class family itself. The second half of the nineteenth century saw the reduction in size of the bourgeois family and a new involvement by parents in the upbringing of their children. The maiden aunt may have lost her role and been replaced by a nanny who could do the tiresome bits without seducing the children's affections. At the same time, middle class spinsters had more chance of survival outside the home with the expansion of public education and the proliferation of good causes. As a result there may have been less need to de-sexualise the maiden aunt by a legal *cordon sanitaire*.

The saga of marriage to a deceased wife's sister is yet another example of the official boundaries of the family being re-drawn in the light of popular practice. There may, however, be a deeper explanation than one which simply deals with pressure groups and public debate.

(iii)   A Hypothesis

In a social formation where marriage is a central device in the transmission of productive property, certain rules governing the range of possible marriage partners must be devised. One of the principles behind the rules of affinity (that is relationship by social ascription rather than blood) will be the need to regulate the flow of outsiders coming into that society or, conversely, restricting the outflow of indigenous members. For example, in some local economies it will be desirable to ensure a regular influx of foreign skills, property and connections, whilst in others it will be desirable to control it.

Although the general ecclesiastical law would not appear to be sufficiently flexible to satisfy differing local requirements, one can speculate that regional customs would ignore or adapt the formal law in the same way that official rules on marriage formation generally were moulded. Historically it is likely that there has always been a gulf between actual kinship practices and religious doctrine on prohibited degrees so that at certain times one could hardly find any marriage the validity of which could not be challenged (Goody, 1983, p. 142). If Goody's thesis is correct that the Church's real interest in laying down extensive prohibitions on marriage between kin was a vested one of promoting the break-up of estates and the circulation of land then that adds weight to the speculation that people will tend to resist it if it is not in their own interests. By and large a small-holding economy will not benefit from regular out-marriage because the means of production become less efficient the more they are divided up. It makes more sense, therefore, to marry endogamously; whatever the Church might say.

As the society moves towards wage-labour and the home becomes separated from the visible productive process, a new code of support obligations may become necessary. Child-raising becomes more markedly the responsibility of those who stay in the home. Should the child-raiser die, a replacement is urgently needed and for the majority of people in limited living accommodation the relationship between the adults will need some public validation. If they are not related by blood, that validation is usually supplied by a form of marriage. In traditionally endogamous regions these new conditions create a further reason for marrying within and consequently a further reason for ignoring the formal law. In urban regions lacking distinct traditions, dependence on wage labour may make necessary a practice of sisters-in-law moving in with a widower, particularly where the sister-in-law herself is otherwise economically vulnerable.

Economic pressures work differently on different social classes, however. The wife's sister can usually only be a substitute for the working class wife whereas she can be an assistant to a middle-class one. Hence in one instance public sanction to a sexual relationship may be required; in the other the existence of such a sanction is seen as a threat to the family's stability if it *encourages* a sexual relationship (or is perceived as doing so). This introduces an element of class conflict into the issue and explains the reluctance of the legislature to validate marriage with a deceased wife's sister.

This hypothesis does not explain why Lord Lyndhurst's Act should have invalidated the marriages in the first place. We do not know whether the Act was a historical freak or a response to more general structural pressures on a section of the country's rulers. In any event, it is unlikely that the new rationalism would for long have allowed marriage laws to remain ambiguous and a common relationship to exist in legal limbo. In all probability, therefore, the matter would have come to a head in that period anyway.

Having suggested why a social practice arguably in contravention of ecclesiastical law may have come about and then been transformed under new circumstances, and why obstacles were placed in the way of legalising the practice, it remains to speculate why a section of the middle and propertied classes should have agitated for reform. I have already suggested that, in part, reform should be seen in the context of moralisation of the working class but that does not take account of the fact that these marriages were not uncommon amongst the middle class as well. It is interesting to note that the private enquiry authorised by the Royal Commission in 1847, which by its own admission concentrated on the middle ranks anyway, revealed that in all but thirty-eight of the reported cases the marriages had taken place in Scotland or abroad. The inference is that the trip had been made for the sole purpose of marrying; a luxury not open to the poorer classes outside the border regions. This may provide the answer. A middle and upper class legislature prior to universal suffrage can label working class behaviour as immoral but when the behaviour is engaged in by a number of its own kind it becomes uncomfortable so to do.

The history of marriage with a deceased wife's sister is, in some ways, a miniature version of the production of marriage laws generally. A social practice exists underpinned by economic and demographic realities; that practice is dislocated from higher normative orders; the dislocation itself can be partly explained by economic and class factors; underlying changes require a reconciliation between practice and law and the form of the reconciliation is guided by prevailing circumstances such as class and gender ideologies.

(b)   The Unmarried Wife

Although state unemployment insurance was introduced in 1911, at its inception it covered only three million workers in the building, engineering and shipbuilding industries. Following the First World War, the insurance scheme was expanded to cover over twelve million workers, which was nearly the whole of the working population. In 1921, the Unemployed Workers' Dependants (Temporary Provisions) Act introduced a system of benefit increases to take into account the claimant's dependants. Section 1(2) of the Act provided for such an increase 'where a female person is residing with an unemployed worker who is a widower or unmarried, for the purpose of having care of his dependent children and is being maintained by him, or has been and is living as his wife'. It will be seen that this provision covered two types of dependants. The first was the woman who was looking after the beneficiary's children, who came to be known as 'a housekeeper' and who need not have been having any form of quasi-marital relations with him. The second was the woman living with the claimant 'as his wife'. She became referred to as 'the unmarried wife'.

The origin of this contradictory term lies in the war pensions scheme of the First World War. Lloyd George, on hearing of servicemen's complaints that their 'common law wives' were not entitled to separation allowance or widow's pension, ordered the schemes to be extended to cover them. The Royal Warrant (in the case of the army) and Orders in Council (in the case of the navy and air force) were accordingly amended. With doublespeak not uncommon in the military world these beneficiaries were known as unmarried wives. When unemployment benefit increases for dependants were proposed in 1921, the unmarried wife was added to the list, albeit tacked on to a subsection primarily concerned with housekeepers.

The parliamentary debates made clear that the addition owed its origins to the war pensions scheme, although a few objections on the grounds of immorality were now raised. Colonel Sir John Grey questioned whether it was not a provision 'in favour of immorality' (*Hansard*, vol. 147, col. 483) but he received no answer. Another member suggested that there ought to be a qualifying period. Lieutenant-Colonel Nall observed that (*Hansard*, op. cit., col. 943):

> Where a couple are bona fide living together, and have done so for a long time, it may be reasonable that they should benefit, although personally I do not think so. After all, the cases are not many and it is as well to draw the attention of the people concerned to the fact that they are living in an illegal estate.

A future Solicitor-General, Sir Thomas Inskip, who was later to be recognised as an ardent evangelical and suppressor of the writings of D.H. Lawrence and Marie Stopes, objected to the use of the description 'wife'. He said (*Hansard*, op. cit., col. 1580):

> It is not the view held by the great body of public opinion in this country and it is certainly not the view held by those who glory in

the name of 'wife' and wish neither the word 'wife' nor the position of a wife to be debased and prostituted even by an Act of Parliament.

Even Inskip, however, was not objecting to the inclusion of informal spouses in the legislation but to their being included in the definition of a wife.

On the other hand, there was spirited defence of the measure. Mr. W. Thorne said at the Report Stage (*Hansard*, op. cit., col. 1579) 'it is only the Parson's fee that makes her a wife' and another member was more forthright. Captain Loseby, responding to a religious objection, said (*Hansard*, op. cit., col. 1582):

> Such references during the war as to the unmarried wife have seemed to me a great advance, and I cannot see any point in such hypocritical, uncharitable objections. I can only tell him, if he wants to refer to 'this odious practice' that it was commenced by the founder of the religion of which he is a member when he said 'Let him who is without sin cast the first stone'.

The following year the system of increases for dependants was made permanent by the Unemployment Insurance Act 1922 and the unmarried wife was again included in the list of dependants. One member, Sir F. Banbury, thought this 'a provision of a slightly immoral character' (*Hansard*, vol. 192, col. 1398) but on being assured that it had been in the previous Act he dropped his objections.

And there matters stood for five years. There is no indication of problems over the interpretation of the words 'as his wife' and there are few papers on the matter at the Public Record Office. On the other hand, there are several files of records on the administration of War Pensions in the 1920s and they reveal a surprising lack of moral overtones on the part of civil servants and others who administered the schemes. Indeed, there remains on the files a letter from the Chelmsford District Local War Pensions Committee dated 6 October 1922 suggesting a change in the rules to *extend* the scheme by allowing an unmarried wife to claim resumption of pension if she becomes incapable of self-support after its cessation (PRO, OIN 7, piece 145). The test for an unmarried wife was said to be that 'she must have lived with the soldier on a bona fide domestic basis prior to the war or to his mobilisation if later' (ibid., piece 150).

In 1925, the first cohabitation rule was introduced by s. 21(1) of the Widows' Orphans' and Old Age Contributory Pensions Act 1925. As a result, a widow's right to benefit was suspended 'if and so long as she and any person are cohabiting as man and wife'. Between 1925 and 1927 the law was consistent in its own way. It recognised, in effect, that a man had a moral duty to support his informal spouse, thus it suspended her own right to benefit and conferred extra benefit on a man when he was out of work so that he could discharge that moral duty. In 1927 this consistency ended. A Departmental Committee, referred to in parliamentary debates as the Blanesborough Report, had apparently concluded that the extension of benefit was a cause of misgiving to many people and was injurious to the credit of the system (*Hansard*, vol. 210, col. 1967). I say apparently because the Public Records Office could not trace a copy of the report and I have not uncovered it elsewhere.

Section 4(2) of the Unemployment Insurance Act 1927 accordingly amended the 1922 Act to remove the unmarried wife from the list of dependants and to make the housekeeper increase payable where the claimant 'has residing with him or her and is wholly or mainly maintaining a female person who has the care of the dependent children'. This new formulation therefore permitted an increase in respect of a female housekeeper looking after his or her children. No quasi-marital relations need exist and the presence of children was crucial.

Although this section passed with a comfortable majority, there was some opposition to it. One member objected that 'the curious distinction is drawn that it is highly immoral for a man to live with a woman and have no children but that it changes its moral complexion and becomes quite right if the lady happens to be fruitful' (*Hansard*, op. cit., col. 1966). Another member, Mr Wheatley, noticed a shift in the moral climate (*Hansard*, op. cit., col. 1970):

> We have an example here of how our morals change. In the war atmosphere we had nothing of this nice distinction. They were all then accepted as quite legitimate wives for the purposes of our Acts of Parliament. Our morality of pre-War days was thrown to the winds. Now that we are out of the War days we are back again into the state of hypocrisy in which we usually live except in periods of national necessity.

I can do no more than present a tentative theory about what was happening here. In the absence of much more evidence, which I doubt is available, this hypothesis may not be falsifiable and could be judged in that light. In any event, one should not discount the possibility of a legislative freak so that the unmarried wife was carried over unthinkingly from war pensions schemes, the policy implications largely escaping notice at the time, but when the area was looked at again the opponents were more vocal. Even this supposes that every member who forms an opinion about a particular issue actually votes in line with that opinion. There are many reasons why this might not be so; for example, the member does not want to jeopardise something more important or feels he or she has said too much already. So the attempt here is to proffer an analysis of underlying factors which is consistent with the events, whilst acknowledging that there might be no factors beyond legislative accident which underlie them.

As far as I know, no research has been published on this topic but Jeffrey Weeks has produced an interesting account of sexual beliefs and behaviour in the period 1924–1939 which might provide a suitable framework. The first quarter of the twentieth century saw a preoccupation by ruling politicians and intellectuals with two related questions of social policy. As ideologies, these can be described as eugenics and maternalism. Chronologically, eugenicist beliefs began to fragment at the same time as ideas about the specific role of mothers in late-imperial Britain came together (Bland, 1982). Both ideologies can be seen as reactions to the social problems associated with urbanisation at home and imperial reverses abroad. The belief that selective breeding of healthy Britons in the right domestic environment would reverse the nation's apparent decline was widespread.

Eugenicist ideas were promulgated by a number of institutions such as the Eugenics Records Office and the Eugenics Education Society, both founded in 1907. On the other hand, these ideas were supported by many outside these institutions. In terms of impact, Weeks argues that eugenics was probably more important in setting the context for policy making than in influencing detailed policies themselves, but a wide spectrum of people from far right to socialist left worked until the 1930s, even beyond, within a eugenics framework.

One can speculate that a general sympathy amongst policy-makers with the idea of regulating the nation's breeding could have influenced the short history of the unmarried wife in the following inter-connected ways. First, marriage by workers within the contributory sector was to be encouraged and if these thrifty types had a rather extended definition of marriage, perhaps inherited from their proletarian past, this could be tolerated. It was those relying on the Poor Law who were not to be encouraged to breed. Second, there was a tendency for eugenicists to use anthropological terminology and this might account for moral relativism over the meaning of marriage. A good example of this is the influential sexologist Havelock Ellis. In his major work, *Studies in the Psychology of Sex*, published shortly before the First World War, he acknowledged that, historically, the definition of marriage varies from culture to culture. He asserted that 'it is the reality, and not the form or permanence of the marriage union which is essential. It is not a legal or religious formality which sanctifies marriage, it is the reality of the marriage which sanctifies the form' (Ellis, 1937, p. 339). In a similar vein, Bertrand Russell's eminent work *Marriage and Morals*, first published in 1929, argued that children were the true purpose of marriage and that marriage therefore only became necessary when children were produced. The similarity between these quotations from Ellis and Russell and that of the Member of Parliament who opined that 'it is only the parson's fee that makes her a wife' (he was speaking about the law) suggests that relativist assumptions were at work in these parliamentary debates, as in others.

In addition to the above ideological points, one can speculate that some of the legislators themselves may have had ambiguous relationships with their own 'housekeepers', which might account for a degree of latitude. In days when divorce still brought disgrace on those in public life, it is not unlikely that the housekeeper was really a euphemism for a cohabitee when the couple were not free to marry. One frequently hears of grandparents and other ancestors who lived alone with their housekeeper in circumstances which are not discussed by the family. It was only after commencing this research did it dawn on the writer that it was true of his paternal grandfather.

If one puts these suggestions together one may have the right climate for a liberal carrying over of war-time 'permissiveness', one consequence of which was the recognition in unemployment insurance legislation of informal marriage. To account for the removal of this recognition in 1927 one must look to the fragmentation of eugenics as an organised set of beliefs and its displacement by new ideas about women as mothers.

If the dominant ideology of the nineteenth century glorified women's position as wives, the early twentieth century accentuated their role as mothers. Colleges of Domestic Economy for Girls sprang up throughout the country and these were welcomed by the authors of one household manual on *Sex* (quoted in Weeks, 1981, p. 127):

Parallel to the admirable revolutionary outbreak of boy-scouting, there is growing up for girls a corresponding novitiate of domesticity.

Whereas in 1904 a classic text on infant care made no mention of the mother, by 1914 maternal care was also advocated (Lewis, 1980, p. 35). Child-rearing became not just a personal duty but a national one and these policies reached a pitch in the mid-1920s when they coincided with the rise of a self-styled movement for 'social purity'. Leaders of this moral crusade included the Solicitor-General Sir Thomas Inskip, who I have already mentioned, the Director of Public Prosecutions, Sir Archibald Bodkin (formerly a member of the Council of the National Vigilance Association) and the Home Secretary between 1924 and 1929, Sir William Joynson-Hicke. One product of these new ideas, I suggest, was a more careful screening of existing and proposed legislation for morally unsound elements; and the unmarried wife would obviously have qualified. A further example might be a Bill in 1927 to remove the disqualification of married women from the professions. The Bill was rejected because many MPs objected that it might lead women to neglect their all-important 'natural duties' (Lewis, 1980, p. 36).

One might argue that six years is too short a period over which ideological shifts can account first for the extension of a legal concept and then for its disappearance and I introduced this hypothesis with the qualification that one cannot discount legislative accident. On the other hand, when one looks at, say, the six years following the election of the Conservatives in 1979 one is reminded of how quickly the terrain can change, particularly in times of social or economic crisis.

4. CONCLUSION

Before moving on to the period after 1945, it might be helpful if I go over the ground I have covered so far and attempt to draw out some of the themes that I said in the introductory chapter inform the study as a whole. The central theme is that marriage is continually being redefined by legal and social practice.

As to legal practice, the State seems to adopt a mixture of, or alternation between, deterrent and assimilative strategies. Its aim seems to be to deter some relationships by withholding some or all of the consequences attached to fully formal marriages but when that fails it selects groups of outsiders and brings them within an enlarged net. The factors which determine the *precise position* of the boundary at any one time—the mediators in the process—are prevailing class, gender and intergenerational relations. Thus Lord Hardwicke's Act was, to simplify it considerably, a response to demands within a particular class to gain greater control over the nuptial behaviour of the young and the deviants within the class. The Civil Marriage Act 1836 was informed by a need to co-opt a group which was largely seen as beneficial to the dominant class but the Act was also designed to acquire greater bureaucratic control over the poor and moral control over working class behaviour, particularly that of women.

As to social practice, I am probably saying no more than that when people form families they tend to act realistically in their own interests. I say realistically because they operate within subjectively and objectively realistic constraints. Subjective restraints certainly include those which the individual could not see through, so that women in particular may form families at the expense of more satisfying ways of living, of their mental and physical health, even of a longer life, but public and male ideologies mask this. Objective restraints include economic dependency and limited access to wage labour and property. So I am not trying to deny the curtailed sphere in which people make their decisions; I am simply trying to acknowledge a space, sometimes gained through struggle, which permits a more free decision. Thus, plural marriage practices up to about 1750, with their possibilities for trial periods, revocation and greater gender equality, were carved out in a way that seems to make some sense. When these lost claims to legal validity, some practitioners continued them whilst others adapted them and created new ones in response to new constraints. When these constraints became overwhelming, for example when the Poor Law Amendment Act 1834 made legal marriage a necessity for many urban women, then plural practices were largely abandoned by many of them.

I present the process as having a legal and social aspect but the relationship is certainly interactive and often dialectical. Social practice will be informed by perceptions of what the law is and legal practice may be altered in the light of social behaviour but often for ulterior or other reasons as well. Underlying it all, as I have said in chapter 1, is the economy; the mode or modes of production. Whilst many scholars may argue about the relationship between and causal powers of economy, class, gender (and I would add generation) I see much less difficulty in locating family formation within the scheme. A predominantly small-holding economy which is slowly being transformed by capitalist relations seems likely to throw up a form of family to which a plurality of marriage practices is suited. In turn people are likely to develop those practices which maximise the advantages and minimise the disadvantages *for them*. A highly stratified social formation at the critical juncture which prevailed in the mid-eighteenth century seems likely to adjust the marriage boundary to increase control. The dialectical process then recommences. Initially, we see minor pressures on the boundary, which might be acceded to, resisted or a combination of the two; the 'unmarried wife' is a good example of this. When the social formation undergoes a major transition, as it did in the mid-twentieth century, and when the economy is restructured, as it was after 1945, then patterns of family behaviour begin to change and the pressures become much greater for adjustments in family law. The following two chapters take up these themes.

5 Welfare, Affluence and the Family since 1945

1. INTRODUCTION

This book has so far sought to explain the emergence of particular statutes that have moved the legal boundary of marriage. Broadly, we have seen the imposition of rigid requirements for formal marriage by Lord Hardwicke's Act 1753 and then a retreat from rigidity. The effect of that retreat has been to convert informal marriage practices lacking legal effect into formal ones with legal effect. The remaining chapters of the book continue the attempt to chart and analyse the legal boundary of marriage but the form of the analysis must change slightly and more in the way of scene-setting is required. Hitherto I have been dealing with highly visible alterations to the law by statutes which were clearly intended to move the boundary of formal marriage. These visible alterations have certainly not died out. Recent amendments have made further provision for marriages of those who are housebound or imprisoned (Marriage Act 1983) and the rules on marriage between affines have been relaxed (Marriage (Prohibited Degrees of Relationship) Act 1986). One could also mention the movement since 1945 towards recognising for English legal purposes marriages which were contracted abroad and which would not have been valid had they been celebrated here. The obvious example of this is the recognition and consequent granting of matrimonial relief in respect of some polygamous marriages.

Whilst these visible developments are not without interest, they are certainly overshadowed by the increasing juridification of some kinds of cohabiting relationships and this process will occupy the remainder of the book. I am looking at the emergence of a body of case law which is arguably having the effect of creating a legal status of informal marriage although it is almost certainly not so intended. In addition, I will outline a number of statutory provisions, many of which appear almost to be afterthoughts, that extend legal rules relating to formal spouses to those who are informally married. Here, too, it is highly unlikely that Parliament in conscious of boundary-shifting when enacting these provisions. Because I am discussing a large number of isolated events which I argue form a trend rather than a single major event it is difficult to use the method previously adopted of moving from general to precipitate causes. The trend itself takes place within a wider corpus of rules known as family law and some attempt must first be made to locate that corpus theoretically.

It may be helpful if I sketch out the argument at this stage and then explain the order in which I present the material. I am suggesting that it is impossible to understand why an informal marriage status is being created without understanding the transformation of family law since the Second World War. Family law has abandoned much of its punitive and negative character and presents an appearance of gender neutrality and non-interference. It is less concerned now with legal status than with economic reality. Marriage is being displaced by 'family' and the wife is being displaced by the mother. Rather than being a primary moral and social regulator, modern family law has become one of a number of systems that demarcate the boundary between the family and the State and its particular function is to contain support obligations within the private sphere. The shift away from a preoccupation with the rights and duties of formal marriage that is involved in the transition from marriage law to family law has created the space for a broader legal conception of marriage. Indeed, if the function of containing support obligations within the private sphere is to be discharged, the law *must* embrace new forms of marriage practice. The gradual and halting juridification of informal marriage that has taken place since 1945 is one inevitable consequence of the change in family law strategy.

In the present chapter I attempt to outline the social, political and economic conditions that have given rise to the new family law. I argue that consumer capitalism and rising standards of living for much of the period have had disintegrative effects on family stability. This instability is potentially compounded by the availability of financial support from the State for dependent women and children. Welfare and family law policies have been designed both to contain instability and to ease dependency from one family to another rather than to the State. In chapter 6 I look closely at changes in family law generally and the emergence of cohabitation law in particular.

Taken together, the two chapters attempt to present a contextual explanation for what appears to be a return to the situation that prevailed before 1754 whereby some couples who had not undergone a formal marriage ceremony were nevertheless subject to legal regulation that did not apply to complete strangers. Whilst these chapters concentrate on State control of marriage through the law, I hope also to bring out continuities between old and new marriage practices themselves. In many ways, modern cohabitation is as much an informed and realistic response to prevailing conditions as jumping the broom and similar customs were in the mid-eighteenth century.

2. WELFARE

Many of the services and benefits today associated with the reforms of the late 1940s actually had their origins in the pre-war period (Brown, 1978, p. 126). Disparate facilities were re-formulated and supplemented by post-war legislation substantially along the lines recommended in Sir William Beveridge's *Report on Social Insurance and Allied Services* (Beveridge, 1942). Although some aspects of the Welfare State are properly attributed to the active initiative of the urban working class (Barrett and McIntosh, 1982, p. 119), it is not correct to see the new scheme as a major victory for working class struggle. As Ginsburg, amongst others, has noted, only in the vaguest sense can it be said that the reforms were shaped by working class values. 'The principal architects of the post-1940 reforms were in fact the progressive, liberal bourgeois who had become committed to Keynesianism and the interventionist State in the crises of the 1930s' (Ginsburg, 1979, p. 9). The welfare state, a phrase coined in the 1930s and later used to point a sharp contrast with Hitler's 'warfare state', was more a crazy-paving than a mosaic (Marwick, 1982, pp. 49 and 63). Nevertheless, it was one of the founding principles of the post-war political settlement and 'marked the boundaries of a consensus within whose limits both major parties agreed to contend' (Hall, 1979, p. 5).

Recent attempts to theorise the role of 'welfare' or 'social policy' have not only provided useful insights on a general, political plane, they have also suggested conceptual tools whereby the relationship between the State and the family can be explored. Common in this literature is an emphasis on how the social relations of production are *reproduced* by welfare policies and this is a useful corrective to the early Marxist emphasis on production at the workplace (see, for example, Cockburn 1979; Gough, 1979; Wilson, 1977; Taylor-Gooby and Dale, 1981 and Pascall, 1986). Social policy can be seen to work both at a material and an ideological level. Materially, it is instrumental in reproducing and maintaining the labour force. Ideologically, it assists in the political reproduction of a working class. I discuss these aspects briefly because I will be making a similar distinction when I look at the family and family law.

The need to reproduce a pliable workforce has been a guiding principle behind social policy since at least the time of Henry VII and, through the use of such measures as the vagrancy laws, probably before. As capitalism expanded it constantly required new levels of skill and adaptability from the workforce and this placed greater demands on the State to improve standards of health, housing and education. The ideological functions of social policy in reproducing the relations of production are equally clear. The acceptance of wage-labour as a natural relationship required concerted State policies in the early nineteenth century and the need to inculcate habits of thrift, labour discipline and respect for private property come out almost as clearly in the Beveridge Report as it does in the Poor Law Report of 1834. These observations on welfare policies may now seem trite but their application to women and the family offers fresh insights and assists in constructing a theoretical basis for contemporary family law.

In many ways, the family fulfils comparable and complementary functions to those of State welfare policies. It is the site where the labour force is reproduced, both biologically and socially, and it 'provides the setting for the unpaid domestic work and caring of women which keeps the cost of servicing today's and tomorrow's workers low' (McIntosh, 1978, p. 155). If it is true to say that the State and the family perform similar functions in materially and ideologically reproducing the labour force and the relations of production then, to complete the symmetry, one can also argue that the State *supports and structures* the family at these two levels. It is this complex relationship which lies at the heart of the theory of family law presented in chapter 6.

At this stage in the discussion we should be cautious about using expressions such as 'the Family' when what we mean is a particular sort of household organisation—the patriarchal family—involving male principal breadwinner, female home-worker and dependent children, although I will later argue that this family form may exist more at the level of ideology than reality. State policies which materially support this model of the family can be briefly stated. The social security system, despite some cosmetic alterations to the rules in the 1980s, is structured around the male claimant. Hence, married women have been able to pay smaller national insurance contributions (which appear to confer no advantage on them) and they have been able to rely on the contribution record of their husband. Supplementary benefit, the predecessor of income support, has been administered through the family unit and, in practice, support is channelled to the man. In fact, the only substantial benefits directly received by women in the family are maternity benefits and child benefits. Whilst these were won after much feminist struggle, dating back to Eleanor Rathbone's campaign for family allowances in the inter-war years, they are, in a sense, double-edged. Both are predicated on the existence of children and therefore reinforce the notion of wives-as-mothers rather than wives-as-women. It is to this ideological structuring of the patriarchal family that I wish to devote some attention.

The ideological aspect of post-war welfare policies has had two facets. The first has been an attempt to structure a clear division of labour and roles within the family. The second has been to perpetuate and nourish the idea that the family is a private sphere, outside State regulation. The first of these has been discussed by several writers (Atkins and Hoggett, 1984, chapter 9; Kidd, 1982, p. 60). For example, Allatt (1981, p. 184) in a perceptive article on gender stereotyping and the law has drawn up a table of social security regulations and their corresponding stereotypes. Thus differential retirement ages reflect 'Women the weaker sex'. Reduced rate of benefit for married women reflects 'Pin money, jam on the bread' and eligibility via husband's contribution record reflects 'Dependent on him, grabbing a man; clinging woman; good worker=good husband/father'.

Some of the gender-biased rules have been slowly and grudgingly removed as a result of European Economic Community Directives or Court rulings (Atkins and Hoggett, 1984, pp. 170–4) although others remain (Pascall, 1986, p. 207; Chatterton, 1987, p. 429) as does their historical significance. If some of the alleged stereotypes seem a little far-fetched then extracts from the Beveridge Report may provide corroboration. For example, we are told that 'the great majority of married women [will be] occupied on work which is vital though unpaid, without which their husbands could not do the paid work and without which the nation could not continue' (Beveridge, 1942, p. 50). The direct participation of married women in the labour market was not envisaged, and this was at a time when about seven and a half million women were in employment (Lewis, 1983, p. 19);

probably only about three-quarters of a million more than would have been working had there been no war (Wilson, 1977, p. 131). Yet Beveridge wrote:

> During marriage most women will not be gainfully employed. The small minority of women who undertake paid employment or other gainful occupations after marriage require special treatment differing from that of a single woman. Such paid work will in many cases be intermittent.

The point to be made here is that Beveridge was not purporting to devise a scheme of social insurance which was adapted to *existing* employment patterns: he was devising a model of how it should be in the future. In other words, the new social security was intended for a new model family.

Of course, the disruption of the war might explain, if not justify, some concerted policy of returning women to the home, if only to increase the birth rate and replace the diminished working class. The influence of the war should not, however, be exaggerated because the birth-rate had been down in the inter-war years (Marwick, 1982, p. 35). Furthermore, the tone of some of the Report is reminiscent of the eugenicist thinking prevalent in the earlier part of the century which I discussed in the previous chapter. After all, the observation (Beveridge, 1942, p. 43) that:

> In the next thirty years housewives as mothers have vital work to do in ensuring the adequate continuance of the British race and of British ideals in the world

hardly sounds like someone only interested in keeping the numbers up; a point not missed by feminists at the time (Price, 1979, p. 5). This emphasis on wives-as-mothers in the new social security system must be underlined because it illuminates what I will argue is a central change in family law in the post-war era: namely, a shift in emphasis away from women-as-wives towards women-as-mothers.

The second facet of the ideological role of welfare policies—the perpetuation and nourishment of the idea of the family as a private sphere—has also received the attentions of a number of writers (O'Donovan, 1985, chapter 6 and Pascall, 1986, p. 25) although it remains a difficult concept to pin down. It is well expressed, however, by Allen (1985, p. 169):

> Much state provision . . . is based upon an implicit ideology of the 'normal' family which through its incorporation into standard

practice effectively discourages alternative forms of domestic organisation from developing. Indeed, by sustaining an implicit, taken-
for-granted, view of family life such other forms tend to be seen as
not simply different but deviant, and hence potentially damaging.
In turn, this allows the state to be flexible and appear non-
interfering yet directive at one and the same time.

There appears to be a contradiction between the claim that welfare
policies have ideologically structured the family whilst at the same
time preserving its privacy. In large part, the second facet is achieved
through simply refusing to intervene materially and allowing social
structural pressures to mould family behaviour (Gittins, 1985, p.
153). When one looks at the material support which the State
provides to families, it is not overwhelming. Child benefit, the
recently revamped married man's tax allowance and the allocation of
public sector housing according to family priority needs are probably
the major examples of material support for the family and whilst they
may be crucial to the economic survival of many poor families, they
hardly amount to significant intervention. On the other hand, the
conditions under which women, particularly married women, can
claim financial support from the State 'have been determined not by a
desire to sustain their incentives to take waged work but by a concern
that they will continue their unwaged work of caring for their
families' (Land, 1984, p. 24; see also Atkins and Hoggett, 1984, p.
162). This argument is a convenient bridge between the material and
ideological role of the State in constituting the patriarchal family.

So far in the discussion, I have concentrated on the social security
aspect of State policy. Education is another major State concern
which plays an important part. Recent work has shown how the
syllabus and organisation of schools help instil into children notions
of gender differences and the naturalness of a particular form of
family life (David, 1980; Dale and Foster, 1986, chapter 4). The
Thatcher Government's concern with the syllabus is motivated in part
by its desire to promote what is seen to be the traditional family
through education. For example, s. 46 of the Education Act 1986
provides that sex education is to be given in such a manner as to
encourage pupils to have regard to the value of family life. Barrett
and McIntosh (1982, p. 30) make the interesting observation that a
common authority structure in schools involves a male headmaster
who is strong, paternal and responsible for physical discipline, with a
senior mistress who has special responsibility for girls and who tends

to discipline by non-physical methods such as shaming. The parallels with the stereotypical family are clear.

Ideological control is therefore the principal means whereby the State can influence allegedly autonomous families. A secondary and related method lies in the practices of those who actually operate the welfare state; largely social security and local government officers. A number of important studies have been published since the late 1970s which illuminate the *application* of 'welfare' to the family (see, for example, Dingwall, Eekelaar and Murray, 1983 and Corby, 1987 concerning social workers and child protection). Two studies which present a neat contrast between theoretical and empirical approaches are Donzelot (1980) and Cockburn (1979). Donzelot's *The Policing of Families* is an historical study of French social policy from the mid-eighteenth century to the present day. He is concerned to note a shift away from government *by* families towards government *through* families. Even after penetrating the opaque, even elitist (Barrett and McIntosh, 1982, p. 99), style it is difficult to know how applicable Donzelot's analysis is to British welfare history. For example we are told (Donzelot, p. 96) that 'the social worker is gradually taking over from the teacher in the mission of civilizing the social body, and opinion polls attest that he has inherited the latter's prestige' whereas the respective status positions are probably the reverse in British society. Further, the psychoanalyst, who Donzelot believes makes the family 'amenable to social requirements, a good conductor of relational norms' is probably far less significant in Britain: although if one extends psychoanalysis to include counselling by doctors (Oakley, 1982, p. 135), social workers, marriage guidance advisers (Morgan, 1985, chapter 2) and 'problem pages', perhaps the difference diminishes.

Donzelot argues that the nineteenth century saw a concerted attempt to 'moralise' and 'normalise' (that is, to instil norms into) the working class. The principal means of doing this was by establishing a direct relationship between women in the family and doctors and philanthropists. In this way, norms of 'physical and social hygiene' penetrated the family. This parallels attempts by the English bourgeoisie to impose their own family form on the lower orders which I mentioned in previous chapters under the concept of hegemony. Donzelot's observations on the twentieth-century strategy, however, are most relevant here. He argues that two distinct methods of moralisation and normalisation have been employed. The first, which he calls 'contract', involves the State establishing a bargain with coping families whereby, in return for adopting a life-style of thrift, discipline and domesticity, these families receive some assistance from the State (for example, through taxes) and little interference. The 'maximum harmony between the principle of family autonomy, its egoisms and specific aspirations, and the procedures of socialisation of its members' (in our terms the contradiction between privacy and intervention) is achieved through the regulation of images (or ideology) (Donzelot, 1980, p. 95).

The second method of achieving 'moralisation' and 'normalisation' is reserved for those families who do not accept this bargain with the State. Here the 'tutelary complex' is employed involving a host of social workers, educationists, criminologists and psychoanalysts intervening in the family. The intervention requires sufficient subtlety as not to 'generate excessive advantage or overly harsh repression and thus cause the old forms of dependence or organic solidarity to re-appear'. The effect of this strategy is to separate out 'problem families' from the rest and reserve the panoply of welfare workers for them. In this way, deviants are contained, those on the fringes of deviancy are deterred and the rest remain unaware of what is going on. The ignorance of most people of the exact duties of social workers is therefore functional: it serves to perpetuate the idea that the family is outside the State.

Cynthia Cockburn's *The Local State* (1979) is an interesting, although unwitting, application of many of Donzelot's ideas. The book is the product of three years' research into the operation of Lambeth Borough Council. Cockburn's concern is to trace the linkages between new methods of urban management and corporate management in the industrial sector. She illustrates how at a time of monopoly capitalism local government is restructured and becomes more clearly an arm of the central State. Her observations on how the local state through, for example, its social workers and housing managers, reproduces the family and indirectly the relations of production are central to my argument, if not to hers. Cockburn describes what she calls the 'local state: family partnership' in Lambeth in which the state is the dominant partner although it cannot do without the family. She shows how housing, social services, leisure and recreation facilities are administered through *families* and not individuals. The mediators between the authority and the family are women (p. 58; see also Dale and Foster, 1986, p. 60):

More often than not it deals with the *woman* of the family. Who answers the door when the social worker calls? Who talks to the head teacher about the truant child? Who runs down to the rent office? The woman, wife and mother,'

The utility of a particular type of family to the local state's administration is revealed in Lambeth when it breaks down. During the 1970s the number of single person households rose from 20 per cent to 27 per cent of all households and the 'standard nuclear family' declined from 36 per cent to 30 per cent (Cockburn, p. 94). The consequences of these changes included unpaid fuel bills and rents and a 50 per cent increase in the number of children in council care between 1968 and 1974. The council tried coercive tactics, including harassment by rent officers and encouragement of tougher stances by the police and electricity board. Interestingly, bearing in mind Donzelot's definition of the tutelary complex, the effect of this was to increase 'old forms of dependence' and 'organic solidarity' which French social policy had sought to avoid. Thus women went increasingly to battered wives' refuges organised on a communal basis, squatting organisations were formed and the mood of hostility to the council increased. The council had then to turn to a 'community' approach involving neighbourhood based Family Advice Centres which could propagate the values of thrift, education and domesticity. As Cockburn says (p. 112):

The FACs worked at the point where the family function was failing. They are the classic example of the local state's intervention in and partnership with the family for purposes of reproducing the labour force (healthy upbringing) and the relations of production (avoiding delinquency, crime and disaffection).

The foregoing discussion has been necessary because of my view that the welfare state is one of the crucial elements in an understanding of modern family law. I have tried to suggest that post-war social policy has operated mainly at an ideological level to structure the patriarchal family whilst perpetuating the idea that the family is outside the State; a private sphere. Much of the literature in this area was written before the Thatcher Government's onslaught against the welfare state and it is worth reflecting on whether Thatcherism's 'rejection of the collectivist political culture that has dominated British politics since at least the end of World War II' (Scheingold, 1988, p. 130) affects the analysis. It is undoubtedly true that measures such as the shift in emphasis from public to private housing and from public to private pension schemes are diminishing that aspect of the welfare state which is replete with familial ideology. Furthermore, removal of many gender biased provisions within social security law and changes to the taxation of spouses certainly makes it harder now to say the Beveridge model family is fully reflected in benefit and fiscal measures. On the other hand, two factors lean against abandoning theoretical reflection on the role of the welfare state. The first is that the apparent content of social policy may change but the practices of those who administer the policy remain. The second is that the Beveridge model family implicit in much of the post-war legislation has played its part in the construction of modern family law, which is my main concern, and family law is now set on a particular path from which contemporary adjustments in social policy could only slowly divert it.

3. AFFLUENCE

Despite the recession of the 1980s, and despite the undoubted existence of poverty and disadvantage in the boom years, the dominant *image* of post-war British society for many people has been one of increased affluence. 'Consumerism', an ideology produced by the post-war boom, has had dramatic effects on the construction of 'the family' in the last forty years. So too has the massive expansion of female wage-labour.

In the early days of the welfare state, social policies and consumer capitalism developed articulated strategies towards the family. Subsequently, however, a combination of hedonism and female employment has destabilised the patriarchal family form and thus created major demands on welfare assistance. In this section, I trace the early congruence between the State's and Capital's view of the family and the growing contradictions in that relationship. I will argue in chapter 6 that family law has played an important part in managing those contradictions.

In the post-war reconstruction, the welfare policies of William Beveridge had their industrial counterpart in the economic theory of John Maynard Keynes. The dominant ethos, according to Greenwood and Young (1980, p. 151), was one where:

the demands of a high production, high consumption economy embraced by all citizens and where the State intervenes on an unprecedented scale to balance out both the economic and moral order.

It would, I think, be more accurate to refer to citizens *in their families*. Consumerism—'the growth in supermarkets, the availability of credit for the purchase of durable consumer goods and, latterly, the use of credit cards for the whole gamut of purchases from alcohol to dining room suites' (Marwick, 1982, p. 228)—comprised a set of ideas organised around a target market of 'the family' (Cockburn, 1978, p. 180). The British boom, as Stuart Hall has pointed out, was confined to the sphere of domestic consumption (Hall, 1980, p. 22). Because the biggest home market in Britain was the working class, henceforth it was *their* demand which dominated commercially. As Eric Hobsbawm has put it, 'Business took over the task of filling the proletarian world' (1969, p. 284), a strategy that did not go unnoticed by one middle class observer in 1962, quoted in Hall (1980, p. 36), who prophesied 'a vulgar world whose inhabitants have more money than is good for them, barbarism with an electric light . . . a cockney teletopia, a low grade nirvana of subsidized, unsupervized houses, hire purchase extravagance, undisciplined children, gaudy domestic squalor, and chips with everything'.

The reference to undisciplined children (specifically, an allusion to teddy boys) was an astute tying together of affluence and 'youth'; a connection that was to be voiced increasingly in the 1960s with the emergence of subcultures such as the mods and rockers. The economic basis for such phenomena has been put well by Stan Cohen (1980, p. 178):

> Before the war, the major spending power lay with the over twenties. No age group emerged—in terms of fashion or symbolic allegiance—in a self-conscious attempt at isolation from the dominant culture. In the years between 1945 and 1950 the grounds for change were laid by a constellation of economic and demographic variables. There was a large unmarried teenage generation (between 15 and 21) whose average real wage had increased at twice the rate of the adults. This relative economic emancipation created a group with few social ties or responsibilities and whose stage of development could not really be coped with by the nuclear, working class family.

The result of moral panics over youth and the generation gap seemed to be a redoubling of efforts to shore up the family and parental discipline (not dissimilar from the reaction to the 1981 riots and football hooliganism). Thus the first strains between the family and the economy were becoming evident.

The home was the prime target for consumer marketing and sales for two main reasons. First, there is the obvious fact that our culture and economy separate the spheres of home and work (although not completely, Barrett and McIntosh, 1982, p. 78) and so people need to consume at home in order to go out next day to work. More fundamentally, however, marketing strategy benefited from a basic division of labour *within* the home. As Andrew Tolson has argued (1975, p. 5) 'the advertisers were able to tap a whole set of traditional attitudes which said it is the duty of men to provide—to be the "breadwinners", to bring home the goodies: and it is the duty of women to take and use what their husbands provide'. Thus, household gadgets were aimed at women whilst, say, cars were aimed at men in which they could be portrayed taking 'the wife and kids' out in leisure hours. The advent of commercial television enabled these images to be propagated with increasing subtlety. The labour force now not only reproduced itself *at* home; it also began to *see* home as the symbol of its new status, as the just reward for effort. So, according to Tolson, 'a universal ideology of home-centred consumption in adverts and the media became one of the most powerful supports for the expanding economy of the 50s and early 60s'.

The deliberate policy of constructing a market out of the domestic sector by stimulating a consumer boom had four, related, consequences relevant to this study. First, the development of new industries on the outskirts of cities entailed the rehousing of old communities and this had consequences for the structure of working class families. It is trite sociology of the family that extended kin networks can survive major resettlements (Willmot and Young, 1957 and 1960). Nevertheless, the greater spatial distance of many housewives from their families of origin intensified feelings of isolation (Elliott, 1986, p. 48) and, to compound their plight, probably made them more receptive, through television and radio, to the very ideologies about 'perfect housewives' which underlay their frustrations.

This leads to a second consequence of the particular course which post-war capitalism has taken; a strategy of stressing the value of motherhood. One result of an expanding economy following a war is a shortage of labour. The British workforce in the 1950s and 1960s was increasingly supplemented from two sources: black immigration and female part-time work. The influx of married women into the economy contained its own contradictions which Stuart Hall expresses well (1980, p. 23):

For consumption to be stimulated, while being at the same time confined to the private and familiar sphere, women had to be located at the heart and centre of the principal unit of consumption, the family . . . But, to sustain this form of consumption at an ever-increasing rate, the wage of the 'breadwinner', traditionally the man, had to be supplemented by the additional earnings of women . . . Women, in short, were being called upon to be both wives-as-mothers—spending home-makers—*and* (part-time) working women.

Women were 'the clue, the door, to this selective penetration of the family and privatised consumption by the "new capitalism"' and they were required to be in two places at the same time. This contradiction was resolved, insofar as it could be, by privileging ideologies of motherhood and domesticity in advertisements, the media and social policy (including family law) whilst playing down women's economic activity. Borrowing from Hall again:

Women-at-work was, largely, a structured absence in these discourses: working was something women sometimes 'did', it did not define what they, essentially, 'were'. Its economic rewards were defined as 'a little something on the side'—'a bit of pin money'. Its true role in supporting the mass consumption boom, and in giving capitalist expansion its appropriate form and definition, was displaced from view.

A third consequence of consumer ideology, in my view, was a liberalisation of laws on sexuality; generally referred to, in the context of the 1960s, by the word 'permissiveness'. The case that affluence and permissiveness were related phenomena is put persuasively by Greenwood and Young (1980, p. 153). They argue that the emphasis on freedom and reward for merit sowed the seeds of dissension:

People took its injunctions seriously, pushing to the boundaries of the ethos and in many cases beyond. Thus workers questioned the balance of the equation a fair day's pay for a fair day's work, women resented the domestic limits set to their liberation, gays demanded sexual equality, bohemians denied the validity of consumer rewards, and significant sections of youth developed their own leisure culture separate from and disdainful of work. The lid was off the pressure cooker and the state was faced with the problem of setting the parameters of the permissive society.

One of these parameters was the new family law of the 1960s and early 1970s, which I will outline in the next chapter.

The fourth consequence of the particular form that the post-war boom took was a new expectation from marriage. Competitive individualism, the struggle for the good life, for satisfying leisure, for the successful marriage, had become major ideals. Geoffrey Gorer, who conducted surveys in the late 1950s and then again in the late 1960s, noted how the proportion of men and women who declared sexual love to be very important in marriage had risen markedly over a decade (Gorer, 1960 and 1971). One result of these heightened expectations of marriage was an increase in its instability. The marketing of romantic love as a commodity led to a view of marriage that could not be realised: hence greater temptation to try again. The high incidence of remarriage by those who have been divorced – about 34 per cent of divorcing people remarry within two and a half years (Haskey, 1987, p. 34) – supports the proposition that the motive for divorce is not simply a desire to end a marriage but also a wish to find a more fulfilling one.

This account of post-war affluence has many similarities with the earlier discussion of the welfare state. At the most general level, welfarism and consumerism were both the products of an attempt to rejuvenate, or re-legitimate, a social order at the end of a prolonged recession and world war. But the similarities go deeper than that. Both attempted to use a new model family—whether to consume commodities or welfare—and both used women to open the door. The welfare state helped to construct ideologically the private, autonomous, self-determining family with distinct roles, responsibilities and powers, whilst marketing strategies played on and reinforced these neatly ordered images. In short, they should be seen as interrelated structural forces.

At the same time, however, the ideologies which underpinned the welfare state came increasingly into conflict with the economic order. Whilst the aim of social policy is to promote a stable family system which can reproduce the working class and the relations of production, the marketing interests of mass productive industry lie in appealing to individuals *through* families. Thus a chain of events is set in motion which is just as likely to be destructive of particular families as it is to preserve *the* family as a stereotypical institution (Close and Collins, 1985, p. 26). This chain of events comprises what I have described as the four main consequences of affluence: the relocation of families in new suburbs, the contradictory position of women-at-home and women-in-work, the demand for relaxations of earlier restraints (permissiveness) and the search for greater fulfilment from personal relationships.

4. THE FAMILY

This section of the chapter looks directly at post-war family behaviour in order to bring out the disjunction between the stereotypical image of the family promoted by welfare policies and marketing strategies and the reality of family practices. I will argue in chapter 6 that it is the tension between the ideal and the reality that accounts for the form of modern family law and indirectly for the juridification of cohabitation. A related purpose of this section is to develop a subsidiary theme that has been running through the book that family practices should be seen not merely as the passive product of social and economic forces but also as conscious attempts to negotiate with those forces and carve out appropriate domestic arrangements. Changing family practices thus exert their own influence on State policy. My explanation in the next chapter of the emergence of a new legal status of informal marriage is intended to reflect this complex relationship between structural forces and human action.

The immediate post-war reconstruction period was marked by 'an intensified ideological "campaign" to return women to their "natural place" in the home, family and marriage' (Hall, 1980, p. 21). It is easy enough to account for this campaign in the context of concern over the birth rate and provision of jobs for the returning troops. Less easy to explain is women's acquiescence in it. Elizabeth Wilson suggests that the Cold War meant women's rights were likely to be associated with masculinised Soviet women and an alien way of life (Wilson, 1977, p. 60). This, combined with assumptions that both the class and gender war were also over, suggests why women readily, if temporarily, returned to the home and 'femininity'. It was probably at this time that actual family practice was most in line with the ideal-typical family extolled and assumed in British social policy. The story of the following forty years is one of fragmentation and diversity.

As economic growth got under way, the demand for labour increased dramatically. That demand was partly met by immigration but more so by the increase of women in paid employment. Figures collected by Webb (1982) and brought further up to date by *Social Trends* 15 (1985) chart this development quite clearly. Between 1951 and 1983, the percentage of women economically active rose from 35 per cent to 47.6 per cent. The most dramatic increase relates to economically active *married* women where the rise was from 22 per cent to 50 per cent of married women. It is true that there is a tendency for married couples to delay child-rearing, and this would account for some of the increase in working wives, however there has also been a significant rise in the number of married women with dependent children who engage in paid employment (given that children are seen by statisticians as dependent on their mothers rather than their fathers). In the period 1981–83, 14 per cent of married mothers worked full-time and 35 per cent part-time. The figures for 'unmarried' mothers (single, widowed, divorced and separated) were 19 per cent and 23 per cent respectively.

The distinction between full-time and part-time work (that is, under 30 hours a week) is a crucial one. In 1971, 34 per cent of female employees worked part-time, whereas only 4 per cent of male workers did so. In 1978, the figures were 40 per cent and 5 per cent (and were unchanged in 1983). During the period 1973–78, part-time work accounted for almost all of the one million increase in the numbers of women in paid employment. As this increase in employment involved mainly married women and consisted of part-time jobs, one assumes that it is married women who do most of the part-time work available.

The relevance of these figures has been suggested earlier and will be reinforced in the next chapter. Some degree of economic independence for women militates against the traditional view of the patriarchal family comprising male breadwinner and female childraiser/homemaker. Thus, in order to preserve the basic structure of this ideal-typical family, strategies were deployed by various cultural and ideological producers to play down women-at-work and privilege women-at-home. I will argue that modern family law played a crucial role in re-legitimating the home as the proper place for women.

(i) Marriage
This brings me directly to changes in formal marriage behaviour. Interpretation of statistics on marriage is difficult because of the number of variables that can affect marriage rates. Most significant of these variables is a change in the average *age* at marriage which makes it difficult to compare cohorts over time and liberalisation of divorce laws which, typically, leads to a spate of remarriages. Drawing mainly on Rimmer's analysis (1981) brought up to date by

Social Trends 15 (1985), the following data are relevant to this study. Since the Second World War, the number of marriages in the United Kingdom has risen and then fallen In 1951, there were 402000 marriage ceremonies. By 1971 this had risen to 447000 but it then fell sharply so that by 1978 the figure was 406000—almost back to the immediate post-war number—and in 1986 it was 394000 (*Population Trends* 51 [1988], p. 48).

As one would expect, marriage *rates* show a similar pattern. These rates, which reflect the number of people in the marriageable age groups and the frequency of marriage at different ages, peaked in the early 1970s but subsequently fell back to their level in the 1920s. The significance of this will appear below when I discuss whether cohabitation is becoming a clear *alternative* relationship to formal marriage.

The combined effect of these developments is a gulf between 'the family'—aptly described as 'a notoriously slippery notion' (McCulloch, 1982, p. 322)—with its implication of universality, and the actual household composition patterns in Britain. In 1985 married couples living with children made up just 28 per cent of households (*Social Trends* 18, 1988, p. 43). The remaining households comprise people living alone, one-parent families, cohabiting couples (with or without children), married couples with step-children of one of them and households containing extended (usually elderly) kin. Furthermore, the married family with husband as sole breadwinner represents only 15 per cent of households (*Monitor*, 1981). These figures support the claim made by Laslett (1982, p. xii):

'The British Family' is *not* the phrase to use, but a phrase consciously to abandon. For there is now no single British family, but a rich variety of forms, states, traditions, norms and usages.

The argument I seek to develop is that the ideology, produced and reproduced in official discourses, that a dominant form of family prevails is a powerful factor in containing further fragmentation of domestic arrangements. In my discussion of social policy I suggested that State practices in social security, education and social work operated from assumptions about family roles and responsibilities and these help constitute such categories as 'husband' or 'wife'. Ideology, by selectively accentuating certain aspects distorts by omission (Allatt, 1981, pp. 178–9) and thus creates a false representation of normality against which people judge the appropriateness of behaviour. In this way, myths about marriage and the family can be widely held and yet be impervious to statistical reality (Brown, 1985, p. 110; Barrett and McIntosh, 1982, pp. 31–4).

(ii) Unmarried Cohabitation

My proposition concerning the ideology of the family may become clearer if I focus directly on cohabitation. The tendency of the courts to differentiate *marriage-like* cohabitees (informal spouses, in the typology I use in this book) from others is a good example of the ideology in operation (Parker, 1987, p. 188). The effect of it is to reaffirm the alleged norm and marginalise the deviation.

There are no wholly satisfactory statistics on unmarried cohabitation. Indeed it is difficult to imagine how there could be if it is realised that one is not measuring a unitary phenomenon. The prevalence of formal marriage can be computed because a definite procedure is gone through and a certificate issued. The couple presumably know what the ceremony is about and pledge themselves to behave in a certain way. On the other hand, the only common characteristic of couples who cohabit is that they share a household. We know nothing about the relationship between them. They might simply be co-residents (for example, 'flatmates') without any particular emotional attachment. They might have, or intend to have, children. They might intend to stay together in the foreseeable future but not want to marry formally; and they might not be legally free to do so anyway. They might also be living together to see whether marriage is worthwhile; in other words a 'trial marriage'. Clearly, therefore, any statistics about unmarried cohabitation cannot be compared directly with statistics on legal marriage.

Allied to this definitional problem are other methodological difficulties both in the research itself and the interpretation of the results. In particular, it is difficult to assess the truthfulness of answers given to researchers. For example, the researchers for the *General Household Survey 1979* (p. 127) attempted to assess the accuracy of their data by probing the answers received about marital status. They discovered that just over half the women who were eventually found to be cohabiting had originally described themselves as 'married'. According to the *General Household Survey 1984*, 70 per cent of the women under fifty eventually found to be cohabiting had initially described themselves as married. Furthermore, the difficulty may not just be in assessing the truthfulness of respondents, but in establishing common meanings. One of the premises of this book is that there may be a variety of meanings about marriage in currency. Someone who has lived in a stable cohabiting relationship may actually believe that it is a marriage, albeit a 'common law' one (Dunnell, 1979, p. 7).

Another problem of interpretation relates to the bias, conscious or otherwise, of the researchers. Oakley (1982, p. 125) notes that:

the collection of statistical data is itself an ideological exercise reflecting the data-collectors' ideas of normality, which are no less, and probably somewhat more, conventional than those held by the population at large.

The *General Household Survey* mentioned above is a good example of this. It is not self-evident why only *women*'s original answers should be tested by the researchers; nor is it clear why the actual findings discussed below refer only to the number of *women* who were cohabiting in 1979. It may be, therefore, that such research is informed by a latent sexism which the *Daily Telegraph*, in reporting the Survey, only made patent by using the headline '300,000 women are living in sin', rather than 600000 people are cohabiting.

Bearing these problems of definition, method and bias in mind, we can hazard some guesses about the extent of unmarried cohabitation in Britain today. According to *Social Trends* 17, 4.2 per cent of women in the age group 18–49 were cohabiting in 1984, defined as 'living with a man (other than husband) as his wife'.

The *General Household Survey*s have attempted to describe the legal status of cohabiting women. It has been found that only 26 per cent of them were never married (that is, 'single') whereas 60 per cent were still legally married and 10 per cent divorced (GHS, 1980, p. 27). One should note, however, that the marital status attributed was that originally given to the interviewer; which, as we have seen, might not be accurate in law. If one looks at the figures from the other direction by breaking down all the respondents into legal marital status (after adjusting for inaccurate replies) and asking what proportion were cohabiting, it emerges that 17 per cent of divorced or separated women and 10 per cent of single women were cohabiting (*Social Trends* 15, 1985).

These statistics, although based on fairly small sample groups, may give some impression of the extent of cohabitation today, but one should remember two caveats. We are not told about social class nor are we told about men. Given that the number of adult men is roughly equal to the number of adult women (Equal Opportunities Commission, 1986, p. 1), then the overall proportion of cohabiting men should be the same. On the other hand, the cultural pattern of men being a few years older than their female partners might make comparisons of age groups unreliable. Furthermore, we have no information on the (legal) marital status of cohabiting men. For example, one might speculate that cohabitees in their late twenties might have a high number of single men living with divorced or separated women because of the tendency of women to marry younger (Equal Opportunities Commission, 1986, p. 4) and thus being more likely to be divorced at, say, 28 than men of the same age. The available figures do not help us.

Two further gaps remain. First, we have no firm evidence that cohabitation has increased over the last two decades. Second, we know little of the meaning of the relationship to the couple; in particular whether it is intended as a trial marriage, or a deliberate alternative to legal marriage or simply a relationship without plans. Some evidence can, however, be brought to bear on these questions.

The first of these matters—whether extra-marital cohabitation generally has increased—is difficult to deal with because demographers were not interested in the question until the mid-1970s. Whilst this could be taken as *prima facie* evidence that there was nothing significant to measure until then, it would contradict the view of those campaigning for divorce reform in the late 1960s. One of the primary objectives of those promoting more liberal divorce laws was to solve what was seen as a problem of 'stable illicit unions' by allowing those whose marriage had irretrievably broken down to destroy the 'empty legal shell' and legalise their existing union (Cretney, 1980, p. 357). In other words, the intention was to re-legitimate the institution of marriage which appeared to be under threat.

Judicial statistics for the early years of the Divorce Reform Act 1969 (which came into force on 1 January 1971) do support this assumption that many people were forced to 'live together' because they were not legally free to marry. One of the new bases for divorce was separation for five years, regardless of the respondent's consent to a divorce. In the first year of the Act's operation, 26.9 per cent of divorces were on this basis and many of those who took advantage of it were elderly. Throughout the 1970s, however, the proportion of five year separation divorces (compared with four other possible bases) fell markedly so that by 1985 they represented only 5.9 per cent of all dissolution decrees (Marriage and Divorce Statistics, 1985, p. 17). An interpretation consistent with these figures is that cohabitation was increasing throughout the 1960s, the Divorce Reform Act then checked the absolute numbers as some cohabitees became free to marry each other, but after these worked through the system the increase continued.

Further light can be shed on this question if we look at some figures relevant to the second problem; the meaning of the relationship. The evidence of widespread pre-marital cohabitation is now so strong that it is possible to start talking about an institution of trial marriage. Of all marriages which took place between 1977 and 1979, nearly one-third were preceded by cohabitation. This was the case with only one in twenty marriages celebrated between 1961 and 1970 (*General Household Survey*, 1979, p. 129). Simply because a legal marriage follows a period of cohabitation does not necessarily mean that the whole of the cohabiting period was a conscious attempt by both parties to assess the chances of a successful formal marriage. It may be that for many of these couples, pre-marital cohabitation is not seen as an intended prelude to marriage but as retroactively becoming a prelude to marriage as the character of the relationship changes (Elliott, 1986, p. 184). One cannot therefore make too much of a continuity between traditional practices of trial marriage, discussed in chapter 2, which *were* deliberate attempts to ensure fertility and complementary economic skills, and the pre-marital cohabitation of today. On the other hand, to assert some parallels does not unduly stretch the evidence.

A closer look at the kinds of people who have lived together before marrying assists us in constructing an explanation of the phenomenon. The *General Household Survey*, 1979, asked the women in its sample group aged 16–49 who had ever been formally married whether they had lived with their current or last husband before marrying him. The answers revealed a sharp difference between those marriages where one or both partners had been married before, and those where it was a first marriage. Nearly half of the former group (that is, a remarriage for one or both) had been preceded by cohabitation whereas only one in twenty of the first marriages had been. If one considers only those ceremonies which involved a remarriage for *both* partners, then 66 per cent had been preceded by cohabitation (Haskey, 1985, p. 16). Haskey argues, by abstracting relevant data, that the marital status of the wife before marriage is more important than that of the husband in influencing whether the couple decide to cohabit before marrying. 'It may well be that divorced wives, especially if they have children, are more likely to have their own accommodation than spinsters, whereas, conversely, divorced husbands are perhaps *less* likely than bachelors to own a home'.

The median length of pre-marital cohabitation differs between groups. Of the remarried group, the period was seventeen months whereas for the first time married group it was only ten months. We can add an age dimension to these figures. Women were more likely to have lived with their husband before their current or last marriage if they were aged 25 or over at the time of the ceremony. Twenty-five per cent of these marriages over 25 had been preceded by cohabitation, whereas the figure was 7 per cent for brides under that age.

'Trial marriage' is more easily measured than cohabitation that does not end in formal marriage. Researchers can easily find the target group—those who are married—and ask them whether they cohabited beforehand. Making useful statements about unrelated adults of the opposite sex who live in the same household is more difficult. Even the term 'household' is problematic in that the element of sharing or pooling, which is regarded as a constituent feature of a household, may be partial or conditional. Furthermore, the sharing may be purely on the basis of economies of scale and not denote any particular emotional attachment (even if this can be satisfactorily defined). Some useful observations can, however, be made about those unmarried couples who have children. These suggest the existence of a recognisable family form which is deliberately alternative to legal marriage. By putting together legitimation statistics and birth registration figures the impression of an increase in this alternative family form can be gained.

Broadly speaking, a child is legitimated if his or her parents marry each other after the birth (s. 1, Legitimacy Act 1976). Whereas 89 out of every 1000 children born illegitimate in 1966 had been legitimated by their first birthday, this had fallen to 55 per 1000 in 1975 (*Population Trends* 14, 1978, p. 14). These figures, by themselves, do not confirm that an increasing number of unmarried parents stay together. If it is the case that single motherhood is now more feasible for women, both in social and economic terms (Finer Report, 1974, p. 249), then this could account for the decline. If, however, one adds the figures of *joint* registration of illegitimate births, the evidence of an increase in cohabiting parents becomes more persuasive, although still not conclusive. In 1966 only 38.3 per cent of illegitimate births were registered by both parents. The percentage has risen steadily so that in 1976 it was 50.9 per cent; in 1981 it was 58 per cent and in 1984 it was 64 per cent (Coward, 1987, p. 24). As Rimmer says (1981, p. 25), 'where births are registered by both parents one can presume some degree of stability in the union'. In 1984, about three-quarters of jointly registered illegitimate births gave the same address for each parent (Brown, 1986).

Statistical evidence can therefore tell us something about pre-marital cohabitation and cohabitation involving children although the two are not mutually exclusive as the couple could marry each other after the child's first birthday and thus falsify conclusions from the above legitimation rates. We have little knowledge, however, of cohabiting couples who do not have children and who do not go on to marry each other. Indeed, one would have to construct a fairly elaborate typology of relationships involving various degrees of commitment (emotional and financial) and stated intentions. In the absence of statistical information based on large samples, however, we can only look to more subjective evidence of the reasons for rejecting marriage and the quality of the relationship. The results of this research may be flawed by methodological deficiencies (not necessarily denied by the researchers themselves) of selection, re-gional and class representativeness and sampling size. Their signi-ficance may lie largely in the fact that common themes do seem to emerge.

The most detailed survey of cohabiting couples in Britain is that carried out by Burgoyne (1985). A sample of 29 currently cohabiting couples and one recently separated couple was recruited and the survey paid particular attention to the couples' micro-worlds. Despite possible over-representation of social classes I and II, the couples' circumstances were largely in line with the statistical evidence outlined above. Thirteen of the couples comprised one or both partners who were separated from their legal spouses or divorced. Eleven households included children of one or both partners. The sample suggested three types of relationship: couples living together as a definite prelude to legal marriage (trial marriage); stable relationships which have evolved and developed from earlier, more temporary relationships and/or shared accommodation; and cohabit-ing partnerships with little expectation—or likelihood—of perma-nence. Interesting information was brought out about the personal backgrounds of the couples. Both men and women tended to come from larger than average families and collectively they had experi-enced a surprising number of disturbing life events before reaching adulthood, such as death of a parent or sibling, parental divorce or a significant childhood illness. There was also a tendency to come from unconventional middle class families. Generally, parents were portrayed as accepting the situation but exerting some pressure on their children, especially daughters, to marry for greater security and, in some cases, for respectability. Those who had been married before were particularly likely to confess they had married 'too young' because of family or social pressures. Many had left home earlier than might have been expected given their circumstances and were thus 'independently' housed and making their own choices earlier than their peers. A central factor in the formation of the relationships was the availability of accommodation. This implies more than the obvious fact that one cannot cohabit without a habitat. It suggests that the ownership of accommodation by one party is a factor in cohabiting rather than marrying. Burgoyne interpreted responses as indicating that a decision to purchase or acquire joint accommodation symbolised a deepening of the relationship. Regarding the couples' longer term intentions, in five cases both planned to marry, in twelve only one partner wanted to marry and in five neither planned to.

As for the couples' micro-worlds and self-images, neither the participants nor the observers in the research found that the partnerships differed very greatly from those of 'ordinary' or 'normal' marriages. Those who were or had been reliant on State benefits were well accustomed to being treated as if they were married. On the other hand, the couples tended to see their relationship as having some differences from legal marriage. It was thought to be more private or self-created so that couples frequently saw themselves as liberated from the scripts, assumptions and stereotyped partnership roles attached to marriage.

Oliver's survey, carried out in autumn 1979, covered seven middle class couples living in the Greater London area (Oliver, 1982). Some significant points which arise from this research are confirmed by Chappell (1982) and Dyer and Berlins (1982). The most important of these is that for young middle class couples marriage may have nothing in particular to offer. At a material level, virtually all the female respondents were in paid employment and could have survived away from home without entering into a relationship with a man. Emotionally, marriage was thought to be claustrophobic, involved fixed assumptions about behaviour and risked greater traumas if it broke down and divorce was necessary. It is probably significant that some respondents lived a fair distance from their family of origin (this happens to emerge from a few of the answers and might also apply to the remainder) and were therefore more free, in a spatial sense, from parental and community pressures. Living away from home, often begun through higher education, is (one assumes) predominantly a middle class phenomenon.

Chappell interviewed three couples; two middle class and one working class. The working class girl was more interested in a future legal marriage than the other interviewees and one of her reasons was the application of the cohabitation rule if the couple ever needed to claim supplementary benefit. Perhaps the middle class equivalent of this was one of the males who was concerned that if a legal marriage did not eventually take place his partner would not be entitled to a widow's pension based on his national insurance contributions should he predecease her. This is a neat example of the stereotypical family assumed in welfare state legislation (of the dependent woman relying on the man's contributions) operating to steer people towards the ideal type.

One aspect of the phenomenon of unmarried cohabitation which I have not yet touched upon is the social reaction to it. At least some of the respondents in all of the surveys I have mentioned referred in some way to 'social pressures', 'convention', 'the done thing' and so on. It is difficult to theorise about this except to say that the dominant familial ideology in British culture is still strongly in favour of children being brought up by married parents. Resisting this ideology is one of the 'social and personal costs' (Burgoyne and Clark, 1982, p. 296) of cohabitation that have to be set against economic gains that the relationship may have. They rightly point out that these costs, in terms of 'loss of respectability' will vary according to the local and occupational community. Only extensive research could assess the extent to which these general statements are applicable to different categories of relationship.

Cohabitation has undoubtedly had some impact on social practices outside the law. British Rail, after pressure from trade unions, extended their concessionary travel rates to their employees' 'common law spouses' (*The Times*, 17 Aug. 1981). This might be seen as the lowly equivalent of the 'mate rates' proposed by several American airlines (*Guardian*, 9 Mar. 1979). At the other end of the British social spectrum, Debrett's *Etiquette and Modern Manners* (1981) now offers advice to perplexed hostesses on sleeping arrangements for visiting 'live-in lovers'. There is, in fact, a serious purpose in mentioning this. It supports the argument that a social process of redefining marriage is underway; a process that parallels the legal redefinition taking place.

Terminology of newspapers is an important part of this process. A pattern is emerging of a differential use of terminology according to the media's approval of the couple concerned. For example, on adjacent columns in one newspaper there were two relevant items; the first concerning a man delivering his partner's baby without calling in a midwife and the second suggesting that gross errors in the Department of Health and Social Security had driven an unemployed claimant to suicide (*Guardian*, 7 Aug. 1982). The first story referred to a 'Man fined for delivering his girl-friend's baby' but the other to the deceased's 'common law wife'. The former case probably had very little public sympathy (although the media themselves could have had a lot to do with this) whereas the latter had a great deal. Another comparison involved a four-year-old girl who was refused admission to a Roman Catholic school because her parents were not married. This attracted adverse press coverage and reference was made in one newspaper to the mother's common law husband (*Guardian*, 8 Sept. 1982). When the school governors subsequently lifted the ban, the same newspaper reported this above a story concerning a scoutmaster who was dismissed for living with his 'mistress' (*Guardian*, 16 Oct. 1982).

Attitudes amongst the general public are less amenable to analysis than those of the media. In 1980, the teenage girls' magazine *19* conducted a survey amongst its readers into 'sexual attitudes' and questionnaires were completed by 10000 readers. Whilst only 10 per cent said that they would *prefer* unmarried cohabitation to marriage, 80 per cent said that they would be willing to live with their man (*sic*) with or without reservations or marriage prospects (Marwick, 1982, p. 254). Clearly these respondents might well act differently if actually faced with the situation and they were, anyway, from a narrow age group. A Mori poll into 'morality', conducted at the same time, disclosed that 50 per cent of the over 65s thought that living together was wrong, compared with only 7 per cent of the 15–24 age group. (*Sunday Times*, 2 Mar. 1980). A survey of readers of a South Wales evening paper in 1981 produced similar 'results'. In particular, 68 per cent of female respondents thought that 'trial marriage' was a good or very good idea (41 per cent and 27 per cent) (*South Wales Echo*, 20 Jan. 1981).

The amount of salt with which these findings should be taken is probably not adequately described as a pinch. In particular, no differentiation is made along class lines. All the rigorously conducted sociological research into marital ideology indicates that young working class girls regard marriage and parenthood as inseparable, inevitable and desirable (Delamont, 1980, chapter 9). In Leonard's study of courtship and marriage among Swansea couples in the late 1960s her informants were able to give very little in the way of accounts as to *why* they had entered into the ceremonial cycle of courtship and marriage. *Whether* to marry and found a family was not the decision: *who* to marry was (Leonard, 1980).

5. CONCLUSION

In this chapter I have tried to lay the groundwork for an analysis of modern family law within which my explanation of the juridification of informal marriage is situated. I have argued that the economic expansion, or consumer boom, which has characterised much of the post-war period has had disintegrative effects on family formation. In many ways this disintegration is analogous to the processes described in chapters 3 and 4 when I looked at the impact of industrial capitalism and urbanisation on marriage practices. Cutting across this simple causal relationship between economic change and family change has been the role of welfare state practices and ideologies. These have attempted to recreate and sustain a family model which seemed to be in jeopardy. Recent family history, then, has been characterised by a contradiction between officially sanctioned family arrangements and the effects of an expanding consumer economy.

Any attempt to fit unmarried cohabitation into the picture should begin with a cautionary note. There has always been a substantial number of people living together outside formal marriage; this whole book is predicated on the notion that legal and social definitions of marriage are rarely identical. What makes the recent evidence of cohabitation particularly noteworthy, however, is that it occurs at a time when legal divorce is more easily obtained than at any time in our history. In other words, we can assume that the unavailability of divorce is now a less significant reason for cohabitation than in the past (Eekelaar, 1980, p. 450). Caution should also be exercised in evaluating how real a 'threat' cohabitation poses to legal marriage. Figures derived from the *General Household Survey* indicate that cohabitation—even pre-marital cohabitation—remains a minority practice and they provide no support for the contention that formal marriage is under siege. Nevertheless, we are witnessing a phenomenon which is significant enough to warrant investigation by government and private researchers and, as we will see, substantial revisions in English family law.

The conclusions I draw from the limited data available are as follows. Welfare provision and increased access of women to the labour market has removed some of the purpose of marriage as a support institution. If the breakdown of a relationship, particularly where there are no children, is not going to require a continuing maintenance obligation, the incentive for many women to marry will diminish. Social class may be an important factor in this process, although none of the surveys discussed above can support anything other than the most tentative conclusions about this. One can speculate that cohabitation might be attractive to two main groups. First, young middle class men and women who are likely to earn enough to be self-supporting and wish to postpone child-rearing have little incentive, other than parental and social pressures, to marry; and the opinion surveys discussed above indicate that these pressures are waning. Second, working class men and women in, say, their late twenties or early thirties may find that their marriages have broken down and they are reluctant to make the sort of commitments traditionally required of marriage. The reason for being specific about the age of this category is because working class men and women tend both to marry and divorce earlier than those in the middle class (Reid, 1981, p. 164). Working class women who have been through a divorce might be prepared to form a new relationship but be slow to remarry. Having come through the traumas associated with a divorce (such as seeing solicitors, attending court to discuss arrangements for the children) they may now be in secure public sector housing with a regular income from social security. The supplementary benefit (now income support) may cease on cohabitation but at least the house is theirs.

Some support for this hypothesis can be derived from the above statistics. The *General Household Surveys* noted that only 26 per cent of the cohabiting women had never married (that is, were 'single') whereas 60 per cent were separated or divorced. Furthermore, cohabitation is far more common as a prelude to remarriage (for one or both partners) than for a first time marriage and the median length of these trial marriages is greater. Thus a connection between divorce and subsequent cohabitation can be pencilled.

The class and gender distinctions involved in this hypothesis are completely untested and derive largely from common sense deduction and secondary sociological evidence. One can speculate that working class girls are more keen on marrying young. They are less likely to find employment which would make them self-sufficient and less likely to have entered higher education. Furthermore, early marriage would appear to have greater social endorsement than in the middle class. If one adds to this the prevailing view that early marriages are more likely to result in divorce, and the higher proportion of divorce amongst the working class generally, one may begin to have a picture of working class women, aged around 30, who have achieved a measure of independence out of a broken marriage and are slow to jeopardise it.

The impression I have intended to convey is one of a growing number of men and women organising their lives in a way that seems to them to make sense. The tension between the State-promoted ideal family and actual practice has grown steadily since the Second World War. One might wonder how the material support given by the State to the stereotypical family, and the messages which State policy and practice send out, have been sufficient even to contain the fragmentation to this extent. In my view, the new family law has been crucial in the containment strategy.

6 The New Family Law

1. INTRODUCTION

In the previous chapter I foreshadowed a view that cohabitation law cannot be subjected to direct theoretical reflection. Instead it should be seen in the context of changing policies and discourses in the new family law. This chapter therefore begins by subjecting that body of law to analysis and isolating two of its dominant functions: these are to further State policies on women and the family and to demarcate the perceived boundaries between the State and the family. These two functions have become more coherent and visible since 1945 for a number of reasons. First, a partial retreat from State concern with private morality has removed an earlier contradiction between public concern that husbands should maintain wives and the competing concern that 'guilty' wives should be deprived of divorce and spousal maintenance. This contradiction led to a confused situation in which it was unclear when the State could recover from a husband benefit paid out to a wife. Second, expanded welfare state policies have offered alternative means of support and accommodation for dependent women and children and so steps have been taken to shore up private responsibilities. Third, and overlaying these factors, the expansion of the labour market has offered some women realistic possibilities of survival outside a family so that blatantly discriminatory policies within marriage law potentially provided real disincentives for some women to enter the system at all. Complicating matters further, the expansion of home-ownership and rapid house price inflation has created new problems of capital division on relationship breakdown.

The result of these developments has been a narrower focusing on the financial aspects of breakdown and a revelation of the underlying economic and financial exchange at the heart of the marriage contract (Smart, 1984, p. 100). At a more fundamental level, family law has become a significant mediator of the conflict, outlined in the previous chapter, between the integrative ideologies in State practice and the disintegrative consequences of consumer capitalism.

The legal strategies that have developed to discharge these two major functions have entailed a gradual displacement of 'marriage' by 'family' and of 'wife' by 'mother' and factual dependency. A space

126

has opened up into which problems on cohabitation breakdown can enter. By the metaphor of 'space' I do not just mean that legal hooks are created onto which marriage and cohabitation problems can equally easily hang, although the law sometimes does develop simply because concepts applicable to one situation are later seen as applicable to another. I mean also that discourses and perceptions of justice have become partially detached from the rhetoric of marital rights and duties so that individual law-makers, either judges or parliamentarians, are at least nagged by doubts when a remedy available to a spouse is withheld from someone else who appears to be in the same situation.

These arguments, which I have presented in very much condensed form, are explored in greater detail in the sections that follow. First I set the scene by outlining very briefly some of the major changes that have taken place since 1945. I then present a conventional interpretation of these changes so that I can contrast it with an alternative approach. The discussion of cohabitation law that succeeds it draws on that alternative approach to explain why the State may slowly be admitting cohabitation as an informal marriage status.

2.   POST-WAR FAMILY LAW

Space does not permit a comprehensive survey of all the changes that appear to have taken place in what is now known as family law in the last forty years or so. Bearing in mind that some readers are not directly concerned with a detailed understanding of the law, and those who are can easily refer to standard works such as Cretney (1984 and 1987) and Bromley (1987). I have tried to isolate significant ideological and policy shifts. In this section I do so without reference to cohabitation law, although developments there should be seen as part of the general pattern, as I will deal with it specifically in a later section.

The post-war period has seen an explosion of law making on family matters. The Legal Aid Act 1949, by providing the working class with much greater access to lawyers and the courts, boosted the downward expansion of the law by enabling large numbers of war-torn marriages to be legally buried (Marwick, 1982, p. 64). There has also been an outward expansion whereby new types of problems have been brought within legal regulation. Four examples follow.

(a) The recognition of polygamous marriages contracted abroad.

In 1965, a serving Law Lord wrote that 'Monogamy is so deeply rooted in our moral ideas that it would not be practicable to contend that the secular law should recognise any other form' (Devlin, 1965, p. 62). Section 47 of the Matrimonial Causes Act 1973 now permits the granting of matrimonial relief such as divorce, periodical payments or property adjustment in respect of a polygamous marriage.

(b) The development of matrimonial trust law. In response to the dual expansion of home-ownership and the numbers of working wives, pre-existing trust concepts enabled wives who had contributed to the purchase of property that was vested in the husband's name to claim a share in the property of the proceeds of sale.

(c) The creation of new remedies against domestic violence. Following the re-surfacing (or willingness to recognise the existence) of domestic violence as a social problem in the 1970s, new powers were given to courts to exclude a violent partner from the home.

(d) The creation of a statutory right of a spouse to occupy the matrimonial home where she is not a legal owner. In some circumstances this right can be enforced against third parties such as purchasers and mortgagees.

In addition to this downward and outward expansion, existing remedies of divorce and financial provision have been radically overhauled. Divorce is no longer based solely on the notion of a matrimonial offence (such as adultery, persistent cruelty or desertion) so that two years' separation can give rise to a divorce if the respondent consents to the decree, as can five years separation, irrespective of consent (subject to a virtually unused defence). Whilst the matrimonial offence has been retained, in the form of adultery, unreasonable behaviour and two years' desertion, in practice the procedure for undefended divorce has converted them into arbitrary legal requirements because most such divorces are processed without a court appearance. In the recent past, the matrimonial offence doctrine had its sting not so much in the granting or withholding of a decree of divorce but in restricting the financial provision that the offender might expect. Opinions differ as to the current practical relevance of misconduct in financial provision and property adjustment after divorce but there can be little doubt that it is far less relevant than hitherto.

So the conventional family law scene in the late 1980s looks radically different from that thirty years previously. A comparison between the prefaces in the first and seventh editions of *Bromley's Family Law* (1957 and 1987) brings this out quite clearly. Furthermore, the changes in chapter headings over this period suggest a move away from a rights-based view towards a functional view of the subject. For example, the legal nature of the marriage contract is no longer organised around words such as coverture and consortium but simply 'the effects of marriage'. Regarding children, 'legitimacy' has become 'status'.

As with much law, scholarly analysis of what Bromley in 1957 was able to call Family Law is still largely devoted to positivist rule-handling. In Freeman's words '[t]here can be little doubt that family law has suffered from the reluctance or inability of its practitioners to engage in discussion of the broader theoretical issues' (Freeman, 1981, p. 133). Much of his own work falls outside this charge (Freeman, 1979; Freeman and Lyon, 1983) and the 1970s and 80s have seen the growth of empirical study into the operation of family law and a multi-disciplinary approach to the subject. Thus, and these are only examples, we now have important information on the actual application of family property laws by divorce court registrars (Barrington Baker, 1977), the impact they have on consumers (Eekelaar and Maclean, 1986), divorce mediation and the legal process (Dingwall and Eekelaar, 1988) and the role of divorce court welfare officers (Murch, 1980). The 1980s has also seen a burgeoning interest in the operation of child custody and care laws (see the works referred to in Parkinson, 1988, p. 28). Good examples of multi-disciplinary reflection on the law are Eekelaar (1978 and 1984), Hoggett and Pearl (1983 and 1987) and the *International Journal of Law and the Family*, established under the editorship of John Eekelaar and Robert Dingwall in 1987.

Much of this scholarship has a critical edge, in particular when dealing with specific issues of social policy, but when it comes to more general overviews that are not explicitly feminist the tendency has been towards rather comforting assurances that, except in those areas where there is no 'right answer', the law makes the best of a bad job. Two themes seem to have been dominant and I outline these simply so that emerging alternative approaches can be better understood.

3. A CONVENTIONAL VIEW

The first of these themes is that family law is pathological only. It was best expressed by Kahn-Freund and Wedderburn in their foreword to Eekelaar (1971):

The normal behaviour of husband and wife or parents and children towards each other is beyond the law—as long as the family is 'healthy'. The law comes in when things go wrong. More than that, the mere hint of anyone concerned that the law may come in is the surest sign that things are or will soon be going wrong.

This view was expounded by Eekelaar in (1971, p. 76) and developed into a more full-blown analysis in 1978 although it is not prominent in 1984. It remains implicit in many standard texts through their lack of attention to any role of law in advance of a breakdown in the relationship. In other words, there is little comment on the proactive functions of family law.

The second theme in much of contemporary family law writing is that the law is now neutral. This too is implicit in leading works through the tendency to take 'the family' as the unit of analysis rather than the children, men and women who comprise it. It tends to foreclose discussion of structural domination and conflicting interests within the family. But the theme is also clearly articulated. Thus Hoggett (1982, pp. 402 and 404) refers to the 'long retreat of the State from the regulation of married life' and argues that any attempt to regulate the conduct of married life or to provide a legal 'buttress' to its stability has been abandoned. The neutrality thesis is most fully developed in the writings of Mary Ann Glendon, notably in *The New Family and the New Property* (Glendon, 1981). In this work Glendon argues that the emergence of 'new property' (Reich, 1964), such as pension rights, employment security, tenants' rights and social security benefits, has removed the family as an intermediary between the individual and society. Thus the attenuation of family ties has made family law 'functional, realistic and neutral' (Glendon, 1981, p. 118). Many of the problems with this view are actually admitted by Glendon but not in a way to cast doubt on the premise itself. She produces evidence of how American women, as well as ethnic minorities, are still excluded from the kinds of employment which carry 'new property' rights and how, through ignorance and fear, they do not make the most of the social security new property rights which are available. In other words, this new property which has brought about the new family law seems to be available to a far smaller group of 'individuals' than first appears.

A further difficulty with the premise is that it may be predicated on an expanding economy and continued availability of new property. This too is admitted by Glendon. After exempting, in effect, women and blacks from her theory, she says in her conclusion (p. 196):

Even for those persons who have relatively clear access to new property represented by jobs and job-related benefits, the job security described here conceals an underlying precariousness. It is true that certain changes in what I have called the legal bonding of the employment relationship protect employees against dismissal for 'bad' reasons ... and, increasingly, against dismissal for no reason. But these developments offer little security against lay-off for economic reasons ... In a general economic crisis, new property rights would become more unstable.

Ironically, at about the time this work must have been in preparation, both Britain and the United States acquired right-wing governments and a recession which brought many of these conditions about.

At a more general level there are flaws of omission. First, social class is virtually ignored as a unit of analysis and Glendon assumes that 'family' means the same thing and performs the same functions for everyone. Second, despite reference to the position of women, Glendon is ambivalent on how women fit into the scheme. In most of the analysis she assumes that the choice which women have regarding marriage is of the same nature as that of men. She does not pose the distinction between a woman's choice of who to marry and a man's choice of whether to marry. Third, the issue of power in society is avoided. Glendon's concluding thoughts are a gloomy prognosis of a new feudalism where each individual is locked into some form of relationship with everyone else: a sort of stalemate amongst equals. This neatly sidesteps an alternative perspective that large groups in many societies have always been locked into relations of dependency, whether it be women dependent on men or workers on capital.

The purpose behind this extended review has been to examine critically the assumptions that underly reflective study by some family law writers. The dismissal of class and gender differences, the belief in legal neutrality and law's benevolent concern to allow people to choose whatever family form they care to, are common in family law writing. I argue that this perspective is a partial distortion of reality, if not, as Freeman (1984b, p. 55) suggests, a complete distortion.

4. AN ALTERNATIVE VIEW

An alternative view of family law requires some mental shifts. The first involves a recognition that it is a specialism which has acquired much of its recent shape and form through construction in law schools since the 1950s. Legal academics have, with greater or lesser reluctance, worked within the long-standing dichotomy in western liberal philosophy between public and private spheres. The family is seen as outwith the reach of the State and so family law naturally involves resolution of disputes between private individuals. Bromley's *Family Law* was published in 1957 and is generally regarded as the first undergraduate textbook that drew the subject together. In the preface to that edition the author says that he reluctantly excluded any detailed discussion of such statutes as the Education Acts, the Children Acts and the National Insurance Act 'which are as much part of public and social administration as a part of family law'. This is a good illustration of the adoption of the dichotomy which was entrenched in law school curricula with the advent of courses on 'social welfare law' which represented the public sphere. As a consequence attempts to draw together more legal rules that directly impinge on family life run into time-honoured (and frequently insubstantial) problems of 'course overlap'. Each year an army of trainee-gladiators is released to deal with the effects of gender conflict within a privatised system created by the State. This is more visible in countries where there is a specialised Family Court. In Australia, for example, the Family Court is constituted by the Family Law Act 1975 and its jurisdiction is confined to matters which appear in most family law syllabi. Britain does not have such a differentiated family court system, although the pressures are in that direction and there is increasing specialisation within the mainstream court structure.

Even if this picture of family law as a social construction is accepted, one should not automatically deconstruct it by sweeping away apparently artificial boundaries. In my view, one must look to the effects that the construction might have. It seems to me that it creates the impression of individualised justice between litigants which masks the fact that the courts routinely process cases within a fairly narrow range of patterned orders. In property matters after marriage breakdown, only a tiny minority of cases actually reach a contested hearing along traditional adversarial lines. The courts are much more involved in notarising administratively the results of private ordering. This opens up interesting questions of local sub-systems of lawyer-gladiators who negotiate settlements on principles that may be relatively autonomous from the guidance given in the minute proportion of contested cases that are reported in law journals and law reports. Although further research is needed into the practices of matrimonial lawyers of the kind initiated by Carol Smart (1984, Part III), my own experience in practice suggests that solicitors, consciously or unconsciously, settle into a handful of formulae. Negotiations between lawyers in the same district are about nudging the case into one of them and filling in the figures. They do this in the light of the law on the books and known preferences of divorce court registrars but there is still a large degree of independence. So 'family law' is a creation which reproduces what is partly an illusion of the State's concern for fairness in individual disputes.

This leads us to the next mental shift required which is to re-locate family law as a differentiated part of general social policy on women and the family. In the previous chapter I outlined some studies that have been carried out on stereotyping in welfare policy to show how State practice works materially and ideologically to constitute an image of the normal family that is independent and involves a gender-based division of labour. I suggested that ideologies were particularly necessary in the post-war period to play down the role of women in the public sphere and define them primarily through the home and motherhood. Put figuratively, the mental shift required is to see family law as *underneath* social policy, as a sub-system, rather than alongside it. The alternative approach I am sketching in this chapter will demonstrate how family law rules in the post-war period have furthered general policy on women and the family. One way of doing this has been through the promotion of the image of separateness, neutrality and privacy that I mentioned above. Another is through ideologies of appropriate gender behaviour within a relegitimated patriarchal family. I turn now to the way that this has been done in England and Wales in the post-war period and I argue that one consequence has been changing discourses and perceptions of justice that have allowed, even required, informal marriage to be juridified.

In an interesting article on family law in Britain Carol Smart questioned whether post-war reforms have been intended neutrally to regulate families or simply to legitimate patriarchy (Smart, 1982). She argued that family law in the nineteenth and early twentieth centuries tended to preclude direct legal intervention in the family and that the control was exercised in a negative fashion. Thus, it relied primarily on punitive threats to deprive wives of maintenance and custody. The matrimonial offence doctrine was therefore an important method of maintaining the quasi-criminal character of marital deviancy. Similarly, the legal disadvantages of illegitimacy were crucial in sustaining the social stigma attaching to unmarried motherhood.

Post-war reforms, according to Smart, have tolerated increasing intervention into the family. The 'punitive obsession' has been abandoned and there has been more concern with inequalities within the family. As a result, the position of many wives has been improved by increasing occupation and ownership rights in the home and legislation offering protection against domestic violence. Similarly, the child care legislation of the post-war period has helped families who cannot cope to transfer the care of children to local authorities. Relaxation of the basis on which divorce is granted and new rules of financial provision and property adjustment have enabled more women to free themselves of unhappy marriages and to acquire a share in the family assets without extensive enquiry into their morality.

The consequences of these reforms has been a transfer of responsibility for women and children away from individual men and towards the State. As a result, the centrality of the marriage contract has diminished. The State, not being privy to that contract, has less reason to distinguish between marriage and cohabitation. It is more concerned with structures of dependency than with how they arise.

The interpretation of this shift away from punitive, negative, strategies accords with many of the points made in the previous chapter on 'welfare' and 'affluence'. Smart suggests that family law reforms should be seen as attempts to salvage the patriarchal family by removing some of the blatant discrimination within the law. Most important of all, recent concern with the 'best interests of the child' has shifted emphasis away from wifedom towards motherhood. Thus, the old language of 'the wife's duties' has to be replaced with gender-neutral terminology focused on the children. At the same time, by stressing the primacy of children's welfare, the law can transmit ideologies about women's proper place in the family without offending the modern ear. Although Smart's article in 1982 failed to take fully into account the part played by judge-made law, it is comprehensively analysed in *The Ties that Bind* (1984). What follows is my own analysis of the work of Lord Denning, the chief architect of the new family law.

It might seem strange to pay so much attention to a single judge, particularly one who spent most of his working life in the Court of Appeal rather than in the highest court of the land, the House of Lords. Lord Denning represented much liberal and social democratic thinking current in academic and reforming circles. (In fact, it has been argued that on the question of 'marital justice' the early members of the Law Commission, following its establishment in 1965, held views slightly in advance of Lord Denning [Deech, 1986, p. 67]). In presenting this picture of Lord Denning's work I take him as typifying and partly constituting the family lawyer. In his work can be found the underlying ideologies in the modern law. Also to be found there are the contradictions inherent in those ideologies (Freeman, 1984c, p. 109).

Lord Denning has conveniently set out his version of events in the second volume of his memoirs for law students. In *The Due Process of Law* (Denning, 1980) he includes ten, characteristically succinct, chapters on his 'ventures into family law' and sets out clearly the view of the family which he claims motivated his major decisions. Central to this is his position on women and I quote one passage at length. Under a sub-heading of 'The Difference' he writes (p. 194):

No matter how you may dispute and argue, you cannot alter the fact that women are different from men. The principal task in life of women is to bear and rear children: and it is a task which occupies the best years of their lives. The man's part in bringing up the children is no doubt as important as hers, but of necessity he cannot devote so much time to it. He is temperamentally the more aggressive and she the more submissive. It is he who takes the initiative and she who responds. These diversities of function and temperament lead to differences of outlook which cannot be ignored. But they are, none of them, any reason for putting women under the subjection of men. A woman feels as keenly, thinks as clearly as a man. She in her sphere does work as useful as a man does in his. She has as much right to her freedom—to develop her personality to the full—as a man. When she marries, she does not become the husband's servant but his equal partner. If his work is more important in the life of the community, hers is more important in the life of the family.

This enlightened sexism—the idea that men and women should be equal in their separate spheres—is elaborated later in the book. Thus a reasonable voice tells us (at p. 201):

This freedom which women have achieved carries with it equal responsibilities. If they live up to their responsibilities, their equality is not only a matter of absolute justice, but is also capable of great benefits to the human race: and of all their responsibilities, the chief is to maintain a sound and healthy family life in the land. To this chief responsibility all other interests must be subordinated.

The more we read Lord Denning's attitudes as he expresses them outside legal judgments, the more some of the themes in the previous chapter fall into place. I discussed there some of the effects that 'affluence' has had on post-war Britain: in particular how increased employment opportunities for women outside the home, whilst essential to an expanding economy, have been disruptive of the patriarchal family. Thus, permissive legislation is passed concerning sexual morality and rights within the family which acknowledges the new state of affairs but preserves the primary definition of women as home-makers and child-raisers. Stuart Hall's idea that discourses in the 1960s treated work as something women 'did' whereas mother-hood was what women 'were' (Hall, 1980, p. 23) could have been written with Lord Denning in mind if the memoirs had then been to hand.

If we look at Lord Denning's major achievements within the field of family law in the light of his extra-judicial statements, we can see the attempted legitimation of home and domesticity taking place. By re-asserting the family as the primary place for women, the attrac-tions of wage labour in the outside economy were being played down. Three sets of legal problems are particularly relevant: first, a wife's right to occupy a matrimonial home where the title is vested in the husband, second, a wife's right to a share in the *value* of the home (in effect, the proceeds of sale) and third how the courts are to exercise their broad discretionary financial powers after divorce.

As for occupation rights, the first major step was taken in 1947 when, as a High Court judge of only three years' standing, he took a completely novel interpretation of the Married Women's Property Act 1882. This Act had established the right of married women to retain their separate property and it provided a summary jurisdiction whereby disputes between spouses over the ownership or occupation of property could be decided by a court. Section 17 of the Act enables a judge who hears such a case to make such order 'as he thinks fit'. Denning, J. took this to mean that 'the Judge should have a free hand to do what is just. That discretion is in no way fettered' (H v. H [1947] TLR 645 at 647). In this case he turned down the application by a husband to exclude his wife from the matrimonial home even though the title was vested, legally and beneficially, in the husband's sole name. In effect, he used a procedural section in a sixty-year-old statute to alter the ordinary law of property in its application to spouses. The case began a long series of attempts to give wives some occupancy rights and involved, at one stage, the creation of a new property right altogether called 'the deserted wife's equity' (Bendall v. McWhirter [1952] 2 QB 466). In the end, the House of Lords rejected this new equitable interest (National Provincial Bank v. Ainsworth [1965] AC 1175) and the use of the Married Women's Property Act (Pettitt v. Pettitt [1970] AC 777) but the Lords' decisions prompted statutory intervention in the form of the Matrimonial Homes Act 1967 (now 1983).

The second set of problems involved wives who were trying to establish *ownership* rights (and not simply a right to live in the home). These cases bear even more directly on my proposition that post-war family law has been a continual response to the threat to the patriarchal family posed by female employment. In 1953, Lord Denning again used s. 17 of the Married Women's Property Act but this time to award a wife a half share in the value of the home (Rimmer v. Rimmer [1953] 1 QB 63). The practice then developed in divorce cases of reflecting a wife's *financial* contributions in the share she was awarded in the home. Eventually, the House of Lords also rejected this use of the Act and substituted a less comprehensible and less flexible part of trusts law.

It is possible that the House of Lords would not have rejected Lord Denning's use of the Married Women's Property Act if he had confined its application to cases where the wife had made substantial financial contributions which could obviously be related to the purchase of the home. It appears, however, that he had become anxious that working wives were being privileged in comparison with those who stayed in the home. He was not alone in this. The Royal Commission on Marriage and Divorce in 1955 and the Law Commission in 1968 expressed similar worries. Throughout the 1960s the courts began to make awards which were seen to be disproportionate to the wife's financial contributions. This increasingly came into conflict with more traditional ideologies amongst the judiciary that the courts were there to enforce vested property rights rather than to redistribute them. A passage from *The Due Process of Law* illustrates this neatly (Denning, 1980, p. 241):

> But there remained one gap. What about the wife who does not make a financial contribution; but does her part—a very important part—by staying in the house, keeping it clean, bringing up the children, and doing the hundred and one things that wives have to

do? Is she to be excluded from any share? Whilst the wife who goes out to work gets a half share in the house? If my broad principle had been accepted—by which the court could do what was fair and just—the judges might have developed the law so as to give the good wife (sic) a share too. But the Lords slammed the door in my face.

The House of Lords' rejection of Lord Denning's approach (in Pettitt, above, and confirmed in Gissing v. Gissing [1971] AC 886) led to widespread concern. The new Divorce Reform Act 1969 was not brought into force until it could be accompanied by new discretionary powers for a divorce court to vary strict property rights (that is, to re-allocate capital irrespective of prior ownership).

This leads to the third set of problems to be dealt with. How was the discretion given by the new legislation (The Matrimonial Proceedings and Property Act 1970, later consolidated in the Matrimonial Causes Act 1973) to be exercised? How was 'the good wife' to be rewarded? The major case which laid down what effectively became groundrules was Wachtel v. Wachtel ([1973] Fam 72). Here the Court of Appeal stressed what is now s. 25(2)(f) of the Matrimonial Causes Act 1973 which directs the court to have regard to 'the contributions which each of the parties has made or is likely in the foreseeable future to make to the welfare of the family, including any contribution by looking after the home or caring for the family'.

Lord Denning's account of the background to this decision is illuminating. He tells us that the case 'is one of the most important we have ever had' (Denning, 1980, p. 242) and that the three judges (Phillimore and Roskill LJJ and Lord Denning MR) took over two months to prepare the judgment instead of their usual two or three weeks.

The actual decision in Wachtel is well known to family law students. The Court of Appeal recommended that as a starting point in a judge's calculation, a wife should receive one-third of the couple's joint income and joint capital. One of the justifications for not starting with a presumption of equal distribution has been much criticised. The infamous passage is as follows ([1973] Fam 72 at 94):

When a marriage breaks up, there will henceforward be two households instead of one. The husband will have to go out to work all day and must get some woman to look after the house—either a wife, if he remarries, or a housekeeper if he does not. He will also have to provide maintenance for his children. The wife will not usually have so much expense. She may go out to work herself, but she will not usually employ a housekeeper. She will do most of the housework herself, perhaps with some help. Or she may remarry, in which case her new husband will provide for her. In any case, when there are two households, the greater expense will, in most cases, fall on the husband rather than the wife.

This reasoning has, of course, been criticised on the grounds of gender discrimination and class bias (the vast majority of divorced men cannot afford housekeepers). On the other hand, one could argue that much of what Lord Denning said has some basis in reality. Divorced women *do* often work a double-shift, combining full-time employment with domestic labour, whereas divorced men generally do *not*. Divorced women *do* often remarry for economic security. To become too animated about sexist reasoning blinds one to the real strategy. This, I suggest, was to facilitate the passage of women from dependency on one man to dependency on another. Only in this way can the patriarchal family be preserved in the face of increasing dissolution of particular families. To achieve this there has to be in circulation marriageable men with more capital and disposable income than marriageable women have. Wachtel, then, is a clear example of post-war family law legitimating and perpetuating the patriarchal family by promoting its reconstitution after breakdown.

Further evidence of this can be found in the Conservative Government's amendments to the Matrimonial Causes Act in 1984. A significant feature in these was a move towards 'the clean break' on divorce, by which is meant more emphasis on capital distribution and restricting future financial contact between the spouses. The public ideology, now that 'women have become equal to men' (Denning, 1980, p. 193), was to encourage divorced women to stand on their own two feet. Thus courts can now impose a clean break on a wife and dismiss her application for maintenance without her consent. Courts are directed to exercise their powers so that the financial obligations of each party towards the other will be terminated as soon after the divorce as the court considers just and reasonable (s. 25A(1)). These, and other significant changes, are discussed by Alcock (1984). If one sets the changes against the background of convincing research that single women after divorce, especially those with children, live in or near poverty (see, for example, Eekelaar and Maclean [1986]) then the measures can only have the effect of making remarriage or informal marriage even more necessary for economic survival (Smart, 1984b, pp. 21–2). As Alcock says (1984, p. 364):

> This legislation should *not* be seen as representing any change in legal ideology or practice towards the dependency of women and their position within the family, *nor* as a mere tidying-up exercise to bring the legal rules of the 1970s into line with the judicial practice of the 1980s. It is a continuation and enhancement of support for family ideology through support for *remarriage*, support which is now getting official government backing.

Early empirical research on the impact of the 1984 changes suggests that there has been 'a momentous trend towards the "clean break approach"'. Furthermore, it may not be taking the form of restricted fixed term maintenance but 'a leap away from periodic support altogether' (Edwards and Halpern, 1987, p. 355).

5.   THE FUNCTIONS OF THE NEW FAMILY LAW

Against the background of this alternative view of family law I can now draw some of the strands together into an explicit statement of the major functions that I see family law as performing and its place in a wider network of regulation. This statement provides the frame of reference for an analysis of cohabitation law.

(i)   Family Law furthers State Policies on Women and the Family by Preserving the Kernel of the Traditional Model and Structuring it in the Face of Increasing Fragmentation
Law and Welfare 'fit together and intermesh' (Hirst, 1980, p. 75). The changing emphasis in post-war family law, intended to legitimate the patriarchal family under new conditions, should be seen as an offshoot of Beveridge's notion that if the State privileges the family unit then mothers can get on with the important job of reproducing British civilisation. Family law's part in the scheme became accentuated during the 1950s and 1960s as the expanding economy provided attractions for married women outside the home.

The first way in which family law furthers State policy on the family is by a general reluctance to intervene. Saying this, however, is not to put forward the neutrality thesis discussed above. Rather the non-intervention policy is there so that *other* power relations can be played out within the family unit. The neutrality thesis thus becomes a legitimating ideology for structural inequality within families. Examples of non-intervention abound. The courts have no effective jurisdiction over property matters until the couple are separated; in particular the obligation to maintain only becomes properly enforceable when the wife is living apart from the husband. Furthermore, there is no obligation on a husband to disclose his earnings and assets to his wife. This facilitates, as several studies have pointed out, hidden poverty *within* the family (see for example, Pahl, 1980 and 1984) and also disadvantages an ex-wife in her ancillary proceedings after divorce when she has difficulty proving the extent of her ex-husband's earnings and assets. (Significantly, a private member's bill to give wives the right to know their husband's earnings [(1987) 17 Fam. Law, p. 79] disappeared without trace.)

When the law does intervene in the family, it does so to the minimum extent required to re-legitimate the traditional family model. I have already dealt with Lord Denning's campaign in family property law. Another example is the flurry of official concern over battered women in the 1970s. When the Domestic Violence and Matrimonial Proceedings Act 1976 was introduced, it appeared to be unconditionally progressive. It enabled the county court to grant non-molestation orders and injunctions excluding a violent male from the home without the woman having to commence other proceedings, in particular divorce. The courts worried about the powers they had been given to 'enter into' subsisting families and have consistently subverted the legislation to cut down their own jurisdiction (McCann, 1985, p. 94). For example they have restricted the use and time period of powers of arrest orders (which are thought to be effective means of making the police take some interest) and they have insisted that exclusion orders should ordinarily be of fixed and short-term duration (Parker, 1987, p. 56). Prior to 1983 some courts were clearly seeing exclusion applications as provisional custody cases, so that occupation of the home followed the likely custodial parent, rather than as means of protecting women against violent men. In an abrupt change in direction, the House of Lords in Richards v. Richards ([1984] AC 174) then disapproved of this approach and said that exclusion applications should be determined by reference to the Matrimonial Homes Act 1983. This Act provides for statutory rights to occupy the matrimonial home and allows the court to restrict or suspend these rights. The Act had not previously been thought of seriously as being useful in domestic violence cases. What attracted the House of Lords was the criteria in s. 1(3) guiding the exercise of these powers. The court must have regard, amongst other things, to the conduct of the spouses in relation to each other and this enables courts to enquire into the wife's part in the violence and dismiss her allegations as insubstantial.

I have concentrated so far on material ways in which family law furthers State policy on the family but equally important is its ideological role. It is this role which contradicts the view that family law is pathological, stepping in only when things go wrong. The stereotypical family which is still promulgated in State policy despite its underrepresentation in reality also forms the spectacles through which those who make and apply family law perceive individual cases. Thus, for example, there is a persuasive argument that custody and access decisions proceed on the assumption that children, ideally, should be brought up in a nuclear family with the mother as principal caretaker (Smart, 1984, pp. 120–5) and this is reflected in welfare reports which are acted on by judges.

The perspective of the ideal-typical family is also class-based as well as gender biased. For example, Lord Denning claimed that Wachtel v. Wachtel was a model case when in fact the husband was a dentist and the children were away at boarding school. In other cases it comes through indirectly. One judge who was deciding whether the husband's trustee in bankruptcy or his wife and children should have occupation of the home said that it might be appropriate to postpone sale if a child of the family was sitting 'A' Levels. On the other hand, 'O' Levels or C.S.E. Examinations would not be relevant because they 'are not in general all that important' (Walton J. re Lowrie [1981] 3 All ER 353 at 356).

But these ideologies should not be seen as only operating when a case comes up for decision. My own guess, which it would be difficult to verify empirically but which is informed by experience as a practising lawyer seeing clients' own conceptualisation of their legal position, is that such ideologies gain currency in general social discourse and practice and thereby constitute notions of normality and appropriate behaviour. The media do report family cases quite extensively and people must gauge their own behaviour and experiences to a certain extent by what they perceive the law to be.

This discussion shows how family law, as a differentiated part of general social policy, structures and supports the patriarchal family. There are, however, contradictions between family law and general policy. The systems are staffed by different personnel and the welfare system, in particular, is more responsive to changes in political control. There is, therefore, a continuous process of ironing out contradictions between the two—of reconstituting the public and private spheres. In playing its part, family law also sends out powerful ideologies about the primary role of men in supporting women and the State's theoretical role as a safety-net.

(ii) Family Law Demarcates the Family/State Boundary to contain Support Obligations within the Family
From the earliest systems of public poor relief, the guiding thread has been the need to pass the cost of supporting non-labourers to a family, or private, unit. This has been achieved by mixing coercion with manipulation of family laws (whether customary or formal). Thus, we are told that illegitimacy only became socially stigmatised after the parish relief systems of Elizabeth I were instituted. Thereafter, it became common for unmarried mothers to be expelled forcibly from the area to prevent them 'falling on the parish' (Macfarlane, 1980, p. 74; Stone, 1977, p. 223). This coercion, combined with forms of retrospective marriage (see chapter 2), formed the basis of a strategy which has its modern counterpart. 'Encouragement' by the Department of Social Security (despite official denial) to take maintenance or affiliation proceedings (Webb, 1988, p. 268) and the cohabitation rule (discussed below), can be seen as equivalents.

The institution of a comprehensive welfare state after the Second World War heightened the necessity for strategies which would ensure that the family took the main burden. It was not simply that the welfare state was *new*, because in many ways it rationalised pre-war schemes (Atkins and Hoggett, 1984, p. 162), but it was *seen* to be new. The awareness that doctors might be a more reliable source of medical assistance than female relatives, that council houses were awarded on the basis of need rather than mother fixing it with a landlord's agent, that the State would tide a 'working man' through bouts of sickness and unemployment, gave rise to a powerful feeling that the family was now less important (Marwick, 1982, pp. 65–6). The new family law was one of a set of official discourses and practices which sought to discourage this notion. Recent encouragement of private health insurance and occupational pensions are other good examples of discouraging a 'welfare mentality' (Taylor-Gooby, 1981, p. 204).

The interface between the social security and family law systems is the concept of the liable relative. Since the Elizabethan Poor Laws a defined set of kin has been regarded as liable to maintain each other.

This means that the State can recover assistance from one of the group. The National Assistance Act 1948, which introduced what is now income support, removed the obligation of grandparents and children to maintain destitute relatives and the liable relatives then became (i) a husband and wife to each other and their children, and (ii) a mother and *adjudged* putative father to their illegitimate children. Significantly, the category of liable relatives is now being expanded by a Government committed to a notion of privacy as part of an overhaul of the non-contributory social security benefits. At the time of writing the details are not clear. It is understood, however, that the father of an illegitimate child is to become a liable relative in advance of any finding of paternity. The question arises whether the Department of Social Security may now put greater pressure on the mother to reveal the identity of the father because they can now negotiate with him without the need for an earlier finding of paternity. Furthermore, liability is to be extended to any person who in fact contributes to the maintenance of the child and who, by reason of that contribution, may reasonably be treated as the father of that child. It is proposed to extend the liable relative procedure to a former spouse of the claimant (previously liability in respect of a spouse ceased on divorce). The practice until the 1988 changes come into effect, and which will presumably continue in an expanded form is as follows. The Department of Social Security only seeks to recover benefit paid to a wife and children where the husband is failing to make any substantial payments. In negotiating reimbursement the Department attempts to offer the working husband/father some inducement to pay by leaving him with more than he would be entitled to on income support. This 'liable relative formula' operates as an inducement to pay because if he were taken to court under the liable relative procedure a magistrate would be prepared to make a maintenance order that might reduce his income right down to what his income support entitlement would be if he were not working.

In practice, the Department of Social Security succeeds in recovering only a small proportion of income support through the liable relative procedure but the history of the principles under which it is allowed to recover is a revealing example of a shifting state/family boundary. In the early days of National Assistance (later Supplementary Benefit and now Income Support), if a wife had committed a matrimonial offence (such as adultery) the National Assistance Board could not recover from the husband benefits paid to the wife (National Assistance Board v. Wilkinson [1952] 2 QB 648). The rationale behind this, carried over from the old Poor Law, was that the husband was not liable to maintain the wife in the private system, therefore it was illogical that he be made to pay for her indirectly through the State system. The origin of such reasoning lies in the punitive/negative approach of family law whereby the stigmatising of marital deviancy was deemed necessary; even if the State had to pay for it through foregoing reimbursement of benefit.

As the concept of the matrimonial offence increasingly came into question in post-war family law, and the true burden of marital breakdown on the public purse became felt, the courts re-appraised their earlier approach. In 1955, the Court of Appeal in NAB v. Parkes ([1955] 2 QB 506) held that the commission of a matrimonial offence by the wife did not *automatically* preclude the recoupment of benefit from the husband but it remained a highly relevant circumstance. Since then the matrimonial offence has officially disappeared from divorce legislation and that governing maintenance prior to divorce in the magistrates' and county courts. The former approach is therefore obsolete. Some contradictions remain, however, and the manner in which the courts attempt to resolve them is a good example of the boundary being marked out. One issue has arisen because of the new policy, discussed above, of encouraging a 'clean break' on divorce. The family capital is divided where just and reasonable on the basis of no continuing support obligation by the man to the woman. In Hulley v. Thompson ([1981] 1 All ER 1128) a clean break settlement involved the husband being absolved from maintaining the children of the marriage in return for an outright transfer of the home to the wife. The Court of Appeal held that the husband was still the liable relative as far as the children were concerned and made him reimburse the Department of Health and Social Security for the benefit paid in respect of the children.

The liable relative procedure can be seen as on the State's side of the state/family boundary. It is far less important than ordinary private spousal maintenance laws, however. These can be seen as on the family or private side. It is here that family responsibility is policed. In any maintenance proceedings, evidence is obtained of the parties' resources. A recurrent question is whether the court should count the wife's entitlement to income support as part of her resources. The effect of doing so would be to reduce the husband's liability (because his wife would then have *some* resources); a reduction paid for by the State. For this reason, the wife's entitlement is left out of account (Attwood v. Attwood [1968] P 591 and Barnes v.

Barnes [1972] 1 WLR 1381). One difficult matter on which the courts have had to decide their own position is how far this should be taken if the order that the court would make after disregarding the wife's benefit entitlement will have the effect of reducing the husband's income below that which he would receive on benefit. This is an issue because if he is in full-time employment he could not claim benefit to bring him up to the State's own poverty line. An analogous question is whether a substantial maintenance order should be made against a husband who is himself in receipt of benefit.

Both these questions centre on whether a person whose income is (or would be) on the poverty line has any spare capacity to pay maintenance. They clearly draw on judicial ideologies about benefit claimants and the extent to which a dose of poverty will bring home to people their private responsibilities. The basic stance of the courts has been that the maintenance order to be made against a husband should not take him below the poverty line (Williams v. Williams [1974] 3 All ER 377) but not all courts have followed this (Stockford v. Stockford (1982) 12 Fam Law 30 and Freeman v. Swatridge (1984) 14 Fam Law 215) and one does not know what happens in unreported cases up and down England and Wales. A recent statement from the Court of Appeal by the President of the Family Division is to the effect that there is at least a serious probability that there will be no margin between the husband's actual subsistence needs and his benefit level to justify the making of a substantial order (Fletcher v. Fletcher [1985] 2 All ER 260). This represents a convenient position by acknowledging the prima facie accuracy of the State's definition of poverty whilst not closing the door on arguments that it is too generous in particular circumstances.

One should not confine the demarcation process to a purely financial or material level. In fact, increasing empirical evidence suggests that private maintenance is of marginal importance to many women; many orders are disobeyed and many involve small sums in relation to income support entitlement (see, for example, the research disclosed and referred to in Edwards and Halpern, 1988). On the other hand, the occasions where the relationship between benefit and maintenance arise offer judges opportunities to send out signals about the importance of private responsibility in preference to that of the State.

It may be that the recommendations of the Finer Committee's *Report on One-Parent Families* (Finer, 1974) were not implemented because they would have confused those signals. The Committee argued that there were three systems of family law (Social Security, magistrates' courts and divorce courts) and that they were not properly integrated. It suggested that the courts retreat from the arena and a State Guaranteed Maintenance Allowance should replace private income maintenance. The State would then be reimbursed through an administrative liable relative procedure. In many ways, this would simply have been a more efficient means of implementing the status quo and would have saved considerable amounts of money spent on courts and legal aid. Its difficulty was that the State would be *seen* as the main provider for women outside the family. In a parallel with the practice of the first half of the century where the matrimonial offence was preserved at the cost of losing some reimbursement, public money continues to be wasted in order to preserve notions of individual responsibility. It has been argued that there was an early perception that the Committee would not produce anything practicable. After it had been working for a year, the Law Commission began working on the matrimonial jurisdiction of the magistrates' courts. Barbara Castle suggested that the Law Commission collaborated with the government to perpetuate the magistrates' jurisdiction and thereby reduce the pressure to implement Finer (Deech, 1986, p. 74).

6. COHABITATION LAW

The material in this and the preceding chapter has been leading towards an explanation of what may be happening in the modern law concerning informal spouses. Why, for example, was the then President of the Family Division, Sir George Baker, driven in 1977 to issue the following deprecation? (Campbell v. Campbell [1977] 1 All ER 1):

> There is an increasing tendency I have found in cases in Chambers to regard, and indeed, speak of the celebration of marriage as 'the paper work'. Well that is, to my mind, an entirely misconceived outlook. It is the ceremony of marriage and the sanctity of marriage that count: rights, duties and obligations begin on marriage and not before.

An answer to this question can be sketched out relatively briefly drawing on what has gone before. There is no shortage of detailed guides to the substantive law on cohabitation (see, for example,

Oliver, 1987, Parry, 1981 and Parker 1987) and one needs only to give a general survey whilst situating the rules within the new family law.

One can now find some reference to cohabitation in virtually every nook and cranny of law which has an impact on domestic relationships (and I am by no means confining this to 'family law'). References appear in statutes as far apart as the Pneumoconiosis Act 1979 (s. 3(2) deals with a 'reputed spouse'), the Consumer Credit Act 1974 ('reputed husband and wife') and the Housing Act 1957 (definition of overcrowding in s. 87). They permeate social security and housing benefit legislation (Parker, 1987, chapter 3) and they are intentionally subsumed in broader definitions (for example the definition of dependant in s. 1(1)(c) of the Inheritance (Provision for Family and Dependants) Act 1975). Cohabitation features in a mass of case law concerning property rights and occupation rights and it is directly referred to in family legislation (ss. 1(2) and 2(2) Domestic Violence and Matrimonial Proceedings Act 1976). It is also built into private ordering, such as many superannuation schemes and it is a significant factor in the distribution of property following divorce (Parker, 1987, chapter 2).

A common explanation of all this is to say that it is a response to the increase in informal marriage. Whilst the growth in cohabitation may be a necessary condition, it is not a sufficient one, however. A fuller explanation is obviously because people think that it is right that these references appear. This still leaves the difficult question of why there has been such a shift in the sense of justice to permit juridification of informal marriage in such a relatively short period of time. Why has the space opened up?

In my view the answer is to be found in the changing strategy of family regulation. As marriage is displaced by family, wifedom by motherhood and the support/dependency structures of the patriarchal family assume greater importance than the legal form it is actually counterproductive to the real purpose of social policy to exclude from regulation a family type that is so obviously here to stay. If income support is paid to a married couple at a lower rate than to two single people then the State loses money if an unmarried couple is treated as two single people. If the allocation of resources, such as public sector housing, ignores informal marriage then the State is manifestly not bolstering the private family (within which children are brought up and women are supported by men). If law-makers are forced to deny what claimants regard as their rights by relying on medieval-sounding arguments about morality then the ideology of justice which gives popular legitimacy to the legal system is severely threatened. Even those judges who have rejected a property claim through preference for individualistic principles of trust law cover themselves by saying that the answer lies with Parliament (see, for example, Fox LJ in Burns v. Burns [1984] 1 All ER 244 at 255g).

In the same way that the ruling class instituted civil marriage in 1836 through mixed motives of increasing regulation and preserving legitimacy, and in the same way that the legal position of wives was improved in the 1950s and 1960s to relegitimate the patriarchal family, we now see a further accession to demands *upon terms*. And the terms are important. It is quite clear that only some kinds of cohabitees fall within the net of rights and regulation; namely those who behave like married people. Every definition of cohabitation in statute law refers to marriage-like behaviour. In case law developments, the judges have paid great attention to whether the couple intended to marry or organised their affairs like a married couple because it is easier then to draw inferences about what the couple intended (Parker, 1987, p. 188).

It is tempting to regard this selective assimilation as a grand conspiracy to extend the repressive benevolence of marriage to those who approximate to it. Freeman and Lyon (1983, chapter 8) in their extended account of cohabitation law and policy come near to doing this. Such an approach overlooks the disparate nature of law-makers; parliamentarians, judges, Law Commissioners and so forth. It also overlooks the haphazard way that the law has developed. There is no single piece of legislation devoted solely to cohabitation; instead assimilative rules ride on the back of other measures which chance to be passed.

In my argument, cohabitation law has come about because the displacement of marriage by family, which has been a feature of post-war British social policy, has brought with it and been a part of changing perceptions of justice. Two recent examples illustrate this clearly. The first is a reflective piece by Stephen Cretney, a retired Law Commissioner and eminent family lawyer. In reviewing his time at the Law Commission he questions whether we can justify attaching far-reaching financial consequences to the status of marriage and says that if we are uneasy about that 'we need to think far more deeply about the underlying obligations of support; and from such a consideration the situation of those living together outside marriage could not sensibly be excluded' (Cretney, 1986, p. 53). The second is

an address by Sir John Arnold shortly before retiring as President of
the Family Division. He notes 'the macabre statutory jest which
precludes magistrates who have a monopoly of directing the maintenance of illegitimate children by their putative fathers from granting a
personal protection order to restrain violence within the household of
unmarried cohabitants' (Arnold, 1988, p. 135). Things have come a
long way for such a senior judge to say that the omission of cohabitees
from statutory protection is macabre.

Before illustrating these arguments by reference to specific areas of
law two preliminary points should be made. First, the looser definition of the family does not embrace only cohabitees. Richards notes
that by the mid-1960s the word 'family' was used for almost any
household that contained one or more adults and children, whatever
biological or social relationships existed within them. 'This much
looser terminology, which grew up in the post-war years, made
divorce seem much less threatening to traditional values, as the two
kinds of household into which most children moved after divorce—
those of a solo mother and children and those with mother and
stepfather—were both now generally referred to as families'
(Richards, 1987, pp. 299–300). Second, one should not overstate the
extent to which cohabitation and marriage have been assimilated in
the way that Freeman and Lyon (1983) arguably have done (Parker,
1984, p. 177). It is more likely to be in its very early stages and its
progress may be halting and subject to reverses. If the day comes
when there is a directly enforceable maintenance obligation between
informal spouses then one can say that assimilation has really arrived
(see, for example, the New South Wales De Facto Relationships Act
1984 which gives a limited right to maintenance where dependency
has arisen because of the relationship or childcare).

(i)   Cohabitation and the State

Two areas of public law illustrate clearly the process of assimilation
and the reasons for it; social security and housing legislation. The
most notorious aspect of social security law is the cohabitation rule
which disentitles someone from income support in her own right if
she is half of an unmarried couple. Whilst the iniquities of the rule's
formulation and enforcement have been rightly highlighted, it is
often overlooked how logical the rule is. Fairbairns expresses this
well (1985, pp. 63–6):

It is an entirely logical, equitable and indeed inevitable consequence of British social policy with regard to women, marriage and motherhood; and its abolition demanded by many feminists, would be utterly subversive of that policy. . . . Abolish the cohabitation rule and you establish the right of a mistress to draw supplementary benefit in her own right. Establish that and you cannot in fairness deny the same right to wives at home with children, be their husbands company directors or on the dole themselves. It is social policy's version of the domino theory: the cohabitation rule is logic's last bulwark against the spectre of wages for housework.

The cohabitation rule is a neat illustration both of the assimilation thesis and the proposition that welfare state legislation is designed to confine support obligations within the private sphere. In effect, a cohabitee becomes an additional liable relative.

Homelessness legislation is a good example of the State bolstering the private family. Part III of the Housing Act 1985 (formerly the Housing (Homeless Persons) Act 1977) lays down conditions of entitlement to council accommodation in cases of homelessness. The policy is that families should be rehoused together. Thus an applicant is defined as homeless if there is no accommodation which he (*sic*), together with any other person who normally resides with him as a member of his family is entitled to occupy (s. 58(1)). Paragraph 2.8 of The Code of Guidance issued by the Government says that this definition is intended to cover cohabiting families. The Act does not, however, stop at preserving the integrity of private families. It is also used to create responsibilities within it. Local authorities are not under a full obligation to rehouse homeless families if they find that the homelessness is intentional. This leads to the question whether all the family are to be held responsible for one member's acts. In Lewis v. North Devon District Council ([1981] 1 All ER 27) Woolf J held that a woman who lived with a man who became homeless intentionally was not *necessarily* disentitled by his conduct or by the fact that he might benefit 'undeservingly' if she were given accommodation. On the other hand, he said, the policy of the Act was that the authority should consider the family unit as a whole and the authority was entitled to take into account the conduct of the other members of the family. It could assume, in the absence of evidence to the contrary, that the applicant was a party to that conduct. If one imagines the position of a woman who is actually, or threatened with being, homeless and who is facing a distinctly sceptical local authority, then the likelihood of her being able to produce evidence to rebut this presumption of acquiescence is remote. This case is not an isolated example (see also R. v. Cardiff City Council, *ex parte* Thomas (1983) 9 HLR 64 and R. v. East Hertfordshire DC, *ex parte* Bannon (1986) 18 HLR 515).

A further condition of entitlement is that the applicant must be in priority need. It is interesting that a battered woman does not fall within the statutory definition whereas a pregnant woman or mother of dependent children does. Here too we see the displacement of marriage and spouses by family and mothers.

(ii)　Cohabitation and Private Law

We have already seen that informal spouses are eligible for protection under the Domestic Violence and Matrimonial Proceedings Act 1976. The Act was hastily drafted and passed when the moral panic about domestic violence in the mid-1970s was at its height. In the previous year the House of Commons Select Committee on Violence within the Family had reported. (Significantly, the Committee had originally been named the Committee on Violence within Marriage.) It had included within its definition of a battered wife 'women who are cohabiting with men to whom they are not married' (HC 553, vol. 1, p. vi). The original legislative proposal was to amend the Guardianship of Minors Act 1971–3 which would have had the effect of linking protection with dependent children. When it was later decided that the legislation should be free-standing the original Bill omitted to mention cohabitees but they were added in an amendment. Again, then, new perceptions of justice alert people to the *omission* of cohabitation from legislation.

So far in this selective review of cohabitation law I have dealt mainly with statutory material. The difficult questions of ownership and occupation rights in the home following breakdown of the relationship are dealt with virtually exclusively by the courts' application and adaptation of non-statutory property law principles. This is an extremely complicated area of legal doctrine which I have tried to grapple with elsewhere (Parker, 1987, chapters 7 and 8). My purpose here is simply to outline two approaches which the courts have taken. The first is an equity-based one where judges try to do what they see to be just in the circumstances. The second is an individualistic one where the courts try to find out what the couple intended the position to be and then give effect to it. The distinction is not actually as simple as it sounds because the whole exercise of extracting the couple's common intention can be permeated with notions of what they ought in justice to have intended. This is so because the courts often have to resort to drawing inferences from conduct as there is rarely a provable expressed intention. The equity-based and individualistic approaches can be seen in cases of ownership disputes, where they are played out through the law of trusts (for example, does the man hold some of the value of the home on trust for her?) and in cases of occupation rights (has the man granted her a licence to remain in the property which survives the breakdown of the relationship?). Hovering above the laws of trusts and licences is an equitable doctrine of estoppel. This can be used where, for example, the man allowed the woman to act to her detriment when he should have known that she believed she was, or would be, entitled to an interest in the property. In such a case the court could hold that the man was stopped ('estopped') from denying her an interest. The two approaches can also be played out in estoppel by placing more or less emphasis on what each party's state of mind must have been.

Undoubtedly the leading exponent of the equity-based approach was Lord Denning. In a series of cases in the 1970s, both on ownership and occupation disputes, Lord Denning clearly gave priority to his sense of justice rather than what the parties intended the position to be. For example in Eves v. Eves ([1975] 3 All ER 768 at 771d) he said 'Equity is not past the age of child bearing. One of her latest progeny is a constructive trust of a new model.' This is interesting not just as a legal proposition but also for his choice of imagery. In a later case (Williams & Glyn's Bank v. Boland [1979] 2 All ER 697 at 703a) when he (probably inaccurately) reviewed the state of the law he said 'Even though the house is taken in the husband's name alone, the law imposes a trust on him by which he holds the legal estate in trust for them jointly in such shares as justice requires'. Lord Denning's sense of justice in these cases was largely an intuitive one and can be seen as a continuation of that which motivated him when he was improving the position of working wives in the 1950s and 1960s. A trust could only be imposed where the woman had made some contribution to the acquisition or improvement of the house rather than having contributed domestic labour alone. In two major cases, Cooke v. Head ([1972] 2 All ER 38) and Eves v. Eves (above), the women had engaged in heavy structural work including wielding sledge-hammers. As Smart (1984, p. 109) says:

It would seem therefore that where indirect contributions are concerned the cohabitee must do more than the wife, indeed she must exceed routine expectations of the feminine gender role. It is clear from these two cases that the courts could not imagine women abandoning their 'normal' roles unless it was on the basis of a guaranteed share in the property. In this way they had proved how serious their commitment to the relationship and the joint home was, and hence their claims to a share in the property were treated seriously.

Whilst this might be taken to show the limits to which an assimilative position could be taken, it should be remembered that the progressive judges in the 1950s and 1960s had been unable to find a way of rewarding the homemaker wife through common law property principles and that statutory discretion had to be created when the divorce regime was reformed in the period 1969–71.

Since Lord Denning's retirement, individualistic approaches have dominated and there is little doubt that cohabiting women fare less well in these cases now (assuming that trial judges actually apply recent Court of Appeal decisions). In the leading case of Burns v. Burns ([1984] 1 All ER 244) a post-Denning Court of Appeal denied any property interest to a woman who had lived with a man for 19 years and had two children by him and carefully distanced itself from Lord Denning's approach (see, for example, May LJ at p. 263e). As I mentioned earlier, the assimilative tendency is a slow and halting one. It is tempting to suggest that cases such as Eves v. Eves are a product of the social democratic 1960s and 1970s whereas Burns v. Burns represents the reactionary 1980s. On the other hand, there are signs that progressive judges may be looking to estoppel to take up the running and circumvent the requirement of a common intention in the law of trusts (Parker, 1987, p. 135).

Two further areas of private law, both concerning death, illustrate clearly changing perceptions of 'the family' and the crucial role of spouse-like dependency. Under various Rent Acts this century, when a protected tenant dies it may be possible for a member of the family to take over the tenancy. In 1950, a man claimed that he had been a member of his deceased cohabitee's family. He had adopted her surname and posed as her husband. His claim was rejected with Asquith LJ regarding it as an abuse of the English language to say that he had been part of her family. It would be anomalous if he could acquire the status of irremoveability by having lived in sin (Gammans v. Ekins [1950] 2 All ER 140). It was easier three years later for a court to avoid the old language of morality when the couple had had two children (Hawes v. Evenden [1953] 2 All ER 737). By 1975 the Court of Appeal was able to find that 21 years' cohabitation without children constituted a family (Dyson Holdings v. Fox [1975] 3 All ER 1030). The apparent criteria for finding a family in shorter relationships are revealing. Thus in Helby v. Rafferty ([1978] 3 All ER 1016) a man failed to establish his claim because the woman had not adopted his name and the couple had not encouraged people to regard them as members of a family. Public recognition was said to be important. Furthermore, the deceased had not wanted to marry the survivor because 'she wished to retain a certain amount of independence and freedom' (p. 1023).

Similar selectivity can be found in cases where the survivor claims maintenance out of the deceased's estate under the Inheritance (Provision for Family and Dependants) Act 1975. To qualify as a dependant the survivor must have been maintained, either wholly or partly, by the deceased immediately before the death. This obviously rules out claims by a survivor who had wholly maintained the deceased but in cases short of that the court has a certain discretion in finding partial maintenance and who did the most maintaining, given that maintenance can be more indirect than the simple transfer of funds. The Act requires the court to consider the extent to which and the basis on which the deceased assumed responsibility for the applicant's maintenance. The Act does not say that assumption of responsibility is a prerequisite to entitlement but the courts seem to have elevated it to one (Parker, 1987, pp. 156–7). This is a good example of the law constituting the family as a social space in which obligations are privately assumed, regardless of marital status. More generally, the Act, which was intended by the Law Commission to cover cohabitees, is a further example of law looking to structures of dependency rather than being preoccupied solely with legal status.

Finally, amendments to the law of children illustrate the displacement of marriage by family and the abandonment of the punitive approach. The law of illegitimacy which formerly applied to children of a cohabiting relationship is being dismantled. The main practical consequence of that law was that the mother had all the parental rights in respect of the child and the putative father was only liable to support the child once an affiliation order had been made. Affiliation proceedings were complicated by evidentiary rules and other requirements which set them apart from maintenance proceedings in respect of legitimate children.

As a result of the Family Law Reform Act 1987 much of this will change. Fathers will not automatically have parental rights. It was originally intended by the Law Commission that they would but it was forcibly pointed out that this would invest fathers by rape with rights. Instead, it will now be possible for the father to apply for an order that he shares the parental rights jointly with the mother. Affiliation proceedings have been abolished and the Guardianship of Minors Act 1971 can now be used for the maintenance of all children, whether or not their parents are married to each other. An interesting rule for the construction of future statutes and some existing ones has also been instituted. References in enactments to any relationship between two persons are to be construed without regard to whether or not the father and mother of either of them have or had been married to each other at any time unless the contrary intention appears. This is a further removal of status considerations.

7. CONCLUSION

The arguments in this chapter have been wide-ranging and I will try here to draw them together. I have built on the discussion in chapter 5 of affluence and welfare in the post-war period by locating the part played by family law in containing the disintegrative consequences of consumer capitalism and shoring up the integrated view of the family that was promoted by the Beveridge Report and later social policy. I began with a brief survey of changes to family law in the post-war era to show that there has been a markedly different strategy from the earlier punitive approach based exclusively on monogamy. I then referred to the conventional accounts of modern family law suggesting that the law is pathological and neutral in order to counterpose an alternative perspective. This perspective suggests that 'family law' itself is a construction that relies uncritically on the public/private dichotomy and should be studied as such. It gives the impression of a differentiated specialism concerned with individualised justice between men and women and deflects attention away from the links it has with broader State regulation of women and the family. I argued that family law should be viewed as a differentiated part of general social policy and, when it is seen in that light, complementary strategies in family law and welfare state legislation can be identified. These strategies are to perpetuate the image of the family as an independent identity whose privacy is respected and that there are appropriate divisions of labour within the family.

I then discussed how significant parts of the new family law came about by dealing with the works of Lord Denning and the ideologies that underpinned them. The purpose of the new law was to update and legitimate the patriarchal family, by removing many of the obviously oppressive rules, and recognise the changing economic position of women. The *form* that this modernisation took prioritised women as mothers and homemakers rather than women as women. I then attempted to consolidate these arguments by stating the dominant functions that I see 'family law' as fulfilling. These are to further State policy on women and the family and continually reconstruct and adjust the perceived boundaries between the State and the family. I argued that as these two functions became more refined there was increased concentration on the economic basis of the family and the need to transfer dependency on breakdown at minimum cost to the State. As part of this, the concept of marriage as a legal status was displaced by discourse about the family and attention focused on mothers rather than wives. These shifts brought with them changing notions of justice which were not dependent on legal marriage. The new functions of family law were just as applicable to informal marriage and slowly a body of rules governing informal spouses is emerging. In this way, the law has begun to treat a further group of people who live together as other than legal strangers. The process by which the State, through its laws, has done this has been the central concern of the book.

7 Conclusion

In the opening chapter I said that I am interested in how and why the law has created points beyond which two people living together in a domestic relationship become subject to legal consequences which would not arise between them if there were no domestic relationship. In other words, why do some forms of cohabitation become subject to legal regulation whilst others do not? A subsidiary theme of the book has involved attention to the persistent behaviour of men and women to resist or ignore officially endorsed ways of living and the relationship between this behaviour and legal change. Rather than summarise the ground that I have covered, I confine this conclusion to an assessment of the extent that any overarching theory can be extracted from the material. I should begin by noting the difficulties faced by legal scholars who have propensities towards theorising in an historical context. Abel suggests that law-making has been of marginal concern to many legal sociologists because it requires a macro-social historical perspective rather than the micro-social, synchronic approach of most sociologists (Abel, 1980, p. 805). This must be even more true for those who have not volunteered for the label of legal sociologist. What follows is my own attempt to make sense of what I observe.

I have tried to show that the legal boundaries of marriage, over time, are produced through contestation and that legal change is not simply a tidying up exercise to keep the law in line with social behaviour in a neutral way. Much of the material in each chapter has concerned the issues that were being contested and their economic, social and political contexts. There are many problems in drawing common elements from the contestations with a view to producing a theory, albeit one derived inductively. The major epistomological difficulty is that central concepts, such as the State, the law, class, gender and family are not ahistorical but are constituted differently in different settings.

Whilst the period I have covered might be regarded as the time in which the modern State emerged, the composition of the State and the contradictions within it are linked to specific historical circumstances. It follows that any attempt to say something like 'the State has always . . .' is likely to conceal as much as it reveals. Similarly, I acknowledge that the notion of 'law' is one which must be placed in its period. For example, one guesses that in the mid-eighteenth century 'law', as we might understand it, did not feature in most people's consciousness as rules emerging from specific political institutions but might be undifferentiated from religious ideologies and the discourses and practices of locally powerful people. On the other hand, middle class people in the late nineteenth century may have seen their world much more as constituted by legal categories: indeed they may have seen law as more systematised than it really was. Following from that, the hostility which some men and women had towards the law in one period may not be comparable with hostility in another period because they were being hostile to different things. There is therefore a danger of ignoring important interpretive contexts in generalising about peoples' relationship with law throughout classes and over time. I could go on to make similar comments about the changing constitution of class, gender and 'the family' but I hope the point is made that any theorisation is based on a large number of contingencies.

Dealing first with legal behaviour, it seems to me that the State's attitude to marriage formation at different times since 1750 has depended crucially on two factors; the centrality of marriage in the transmission of power and wealth and dominant ideologies about women and the family. The *form* in which this attitude is translated into regulation is determined by a wider set of circumstances. Principal amongst these are prevailing hegemonic strategies and the extent to which respect for 'law' is seen to be important. In chapters 2 and 3 I argued that until the mid-eighteenth century landed classes were prepared to allow the Church to define the basis of marriage entry and they then controlled those consequences of marriage which were relevant to them by insisting on certain formalities if property rights and legitimacy were to follow. Although there had been attempts for over two centuries to strengthen the formal require- ments of marriage entry, by and large this approach was sufficient to control their younger generation. By about 1750 things had changed, largely because of an increased perception of deviancy within their classes which current measures were not controlling. The use of *generalised* law to control marriage entry was partly prompted by changing class relationships and hegemonic strategies to constitute a new social order. Lord Hardwicke's Act should be seen as part of an attack on popular customs and a desire to reach down into all aspects of social life to produce a compliant populace.

By 1836 the scene had changed again. Landed property was less central to capital accumulation and the panic concerning loss of control over its transmission had diminished. New conditions required that respectable dissenters be accommodated. The bureaucratic state required a system of births', deaths' and marriages' registration that might be fatally flawed if significant sections of the population remained outside the system. New ways of reaching down into social life were opened up by measures such as the Poor Law Amendment Act 1834. Indeed, if the micro-world of the bourgeoisie was to be reproduced in the urban working class then easy access to legal marriage was probably seen as a prerequisite.

In the saga over marriage with a deceased wife's sister a different kind of dissent had to be bought off. Here, significant sections of the middle class were visibly engaging in ceremonies that had no legal effect. The price could be paid because the maiden aunt, who previously had had to be desexualised for fear of domestic disruption, was much less of a stylised presence by the end of the nineteenth century. More concerted attempts to embourgeoise the working class family also depended on the family being constituted by law. There seems now to be more concern with preserving the legitimacy of law itself. Open flouting of the law—'bringing it into disrepute'—was more readily translated into an attack on the fabric of the social formation.

From about the mid-nineteenth century, then, the need to police the transmission of capital through legal control over marriage entry had diminished and concern over the constitution of the family and acceptance of law had become prominent. Many of the measures which flowed from this are outside the scope of this book and more work of a theoretical kind is needed on the history of divorce, the matrimonial offence in the magistrates' courts and family property law in general. In my examination of family law since 1945 I tried to take up this theme in order to explain why informal marriage is slowly being juridified. Although legal revolutions rarely take place in a neat form, the emergence of a new family law in the space of about thirty years involved, at the least, significant discontinuities from the past. The kind of welfare state that was established was predicated on a particular family form that would take the brunt of dependency. Social policy, through its practices and ideologies, attempted to promote that family form at a general level but its hold was fragile. The kind of economy that the welfare state was intended to serve actually worked against a stable family system and a more differentiated and targeted regulatory network was needed to contain and dissipate the tensions. This, in my view, explains the basic form and content of the new family law.

Its first task was to re-legitimate the idea of home and family; an idea which was perceived, rightly or wrongly, as being in jeopardy. Given the apparent opportunities being opened up for women through the workforce and State benefits, measures were required which recognised, but played down, their new status. I described the works of Lord Denning as attempts to do precisely this. On the other hand, actual family instability and increased gender conflict could not be ignored. Strategies had to be developed to recognise that divorce was here to stay and, if long-term dependency on the State was to be avoided, repartnering had to be facilitated. During this time, discourses about 'marriage' gave way to discourses about 'family'. Undoubtedly they were often used as synonyms but slowly 'family' became the larger of two concentric circles and marriage the smaller.

Given the fragmentation of family practices in this time such linguistic and conceptual shifts were inevitable. The most important policy goals are to define women primarily through the home and to protect the private sphere. Attention to substance rather than form has led to new conceptions of family justice. Earlier punitive and negative stances are perceived as outmoded. If a woman lives with a man as his wife then arguments that she should be treated differently from a wife look weaker and weaker. In chapter 6 I suggested that one must not exaggerate the extent of assimilation and the tendency is halting and subject to reverses. On the other hand, the prolifieration of deemed marriage provisions makes it hard to deny that the tendency exists.

The subsidiary theme of the book has concerned the behaviour of men and women in ignoring and resisting State-sanctioned ways of living together. I have tried throughout to preserve some space for human agency and to sketch out a dialectical relationship between social practice and legal regulation. I hope that it has become clear that there have always been significant minorities who have lived without marriage. It was not something that stopped in ancient Rome to be revived in the 1960s. I have tried to stop short of suggesting that modern cohabitees are in any way conscious successors to earlier traditions. Those who live together must be placed in their times and dealt with in gender and class terms. Nevertheless, a common feature is the attempt to carve out a mode of living which maximises advantages and minimises disadvantages. The scope for doing so is limited by practical considerations, such as the law, and any choices are informed by dominant ideologies and social pressures. The choices are also different for men and women.

At the end of the day, if the law seeks to regulate family behaviour (which, despite rhetoric to the contrary, it does) then any response to new behaviour is conditioned by the need to preserve popular acceptance of law generally. If regulation of family matters becomes seriously out of line with the aspirations of significant numbers of men and women then they might regard all law as asinine. Whilst some of the best examples of this are outside my concerns here (I have in mind official disquiet over collusion and perjury which accompanied the matrimonial offence basis of earlier divorce laws) the reasons for acceding to pressure for changes in marriage law also bear this out.

Bringing the legal and human themes together, I have tried to show that the commonplace cosy picture of law following discreetly behind social practice is simplistic. Whilst laws frequently have to be adapted to preserve the legitimacy of regulation generally, or for other strategic reasons, the adaptations are on terms which protect the State's interest in constructing the boundaries of marriage.

References

Abel, R.L. (1980), 'Redirecting Social Studies of Law', *Law and Society Review*, 14, 805.

Alcock, P. (1984), 'Remuneration or Remarriage? The Matrimonial and Financial Proceedings Act', *Journal of Law and Society*, 11, 357.

Alderman, G. (1986), *Modern Britain 1700–1983* (London: Croom Helm).

Alexander, S. (1982), 'Women's Work in Nineteenth Century London: a Study of the Years 1820–50', in Whitelegg, E. (ed.), *The Changing Experience of Women* (Oxford: Martin Robertson).

Allatt, P. (1981), 'Stereotyping: Familism in the Law', in Fryer, B. *et al.* (eds), Law, State and Society (London: Croom Helm).

Allen, G. (1985), *Family Life* (Oxford: Blackwell).

Anderson, M. (1974), *Family Structure in Nineteenth Century Lancashire* (Cambridge University Press).

Anderson, M. (1980), *Approaches to the History of the Western Family 1500–1914* (London: Macmillan).

Anderson, N.F. (1982), 'The "Marriage with a Deceased Wife's Sister Bill" Controversy', *Journal of British Studies*, 21, 67.

Anderson, O. (1975), 'The Incidence of Civil Marriage in Victorian England and Wales', *Past and Present*, 69, 50.

Arnold, J.C. (1950), 'The Marriage Law of England', *Quarterly Review*, 288, 486.

Arnold, Sir John (1988), 'Family Law Conference 1987', *Family Law*, 18, 135.

Atkins, S. and Hoggett, B. (1984), *Women and the Law* (Oxford: Blackwell).

Baker, D. (1973), *Sanctity and Secularity* (Oxford: Blackwell).

Baker, J.H. (1979), *An Introduction to English Legal History* (London: Butterworths).

Baker, M. (1977), *Wedding Customs and Folklore* (Newton Abbot: David & Charles).

Banks, J.A. (1967), 'Population Change and the Victorian City', *Victorian Studies*, xi, 277.

Barrett, M. and McIntosh, M. (1982), *The Anti-Social Family* (London: Verso).

Barrington Baker, W. (1977), *The Matrimonial Jurisdiction of Registrars* (Oxford: Centre for Socio-Legal Studies).

Barton, C. (1985), *Cohabitation Contracts* (Aldershot: Gower).

Behrman, C.F. (1968), 'The Annual Blister: a Sidelight on Victorian Social and Parliamentary History', *Victorian Studies*, xi, 483.

Bennett, A. (1839), *The History of Dissenters 1808–1838* (London).

Beveridge, Sir W. (1942), *Report on Social Insurance and Allied Services* (London: HMSO).

Bickley, A.C. (1902), 'Notes on a Custom at Woking', *The Home Counties Magazine*, iv, 25.

Blackstone, Sir W. (1857), *Commentaries on the Laws of England* (London).

Bland, L. (1982), '"Guardians of the race" or "Vampires upon the nation's health"? Female Sexuality and its Regulation in early Twentieth Century Britain', in Whitelegg, E. (ed.), *The Changing Experience of Women* (Oxford: Martin Robertson).

Bloom, J.H. (1929), *Folklore, Old Customs and Superstitions in Shakespeare's England* (London).

Bonfield, L. (1983), *Marriage Settlements 1601–1740* (Cambridge University Press).

Booth, C. (1902–3), *Life and Labour of the London Poor* (London: Macmillan).

Bradley, L. (1973), 'Common Law Marriage, a Possible Case of Under-Registration', *Population Studies*, 10, 43.

Branca, P. (1978), *Women in Europe since 1750* (London: Croom Helm).

Briggs, M. and Jordan, P. (1954), *Economic History of England* (London: University Tutorial Press).

Bromley, P. (1957), *Family Law*, 1st edn (London: Butterworths).

Bromley, P. and Lowe, N.V. (1987), *Bromley's Family Law*, 7th edn (London: Butterworths).

Brown, A. (1986), 'Family Circumstances of Young Children', *Population Trends* 43 (London: HMSO).

Brown, B. (1986), Review of, *inter alia*, O'Donovan (1985), *Journal of Law and Society*, 13, 433.

Brown, J. (1978), 'Social Control and the Modernisation of Social Policy 1880–1929', in Thane, P. (ed.), *The Origins of British Social Policy* (London: Croom Helm).

Brown, J., Comber, M., Gibson, K. and Howard, S. (1985), 'Marriage and "the Family"', in Abrams, M. *et al.* (eds), *Values and Social Change in Britain* (London: Macmillan).

Brown, R.L. (1981), 'The Rise and Fall of the Fleet Marriages', in Outhwaite, R.B. (ed.), *Marriage and Society* (London: Europa).

Burgoyne, J. (1985), *Cohabitation and Contemporary Family Life* (ESRC End of Grant Report, unpublished).

Burgoyne, J. and Clark, D. (1982), 'Reconstituted Families', in Rappoport, R.N. *et al.* (eds), *Families in Britain* (London: Routledge and Kegan Paul).

Burns, J.S. (1845), *The History of the Fleet Marriages* (London).

Butlin, R.A. (1982), *The Transformation of Rural England c. 1580–1800. A Study of Historical Geography* (Oxford University Press).

Campbell, Lord John (1846), *The Lives of the Lord Chancellors* (London).

Chappell, H. (1982), 'Not the Marrying Kind?', *New Society*, 20th May, 295.

Chatterton, D. (1987), 'Equal Treatment in Social Security Benefits—An Update', *Family Law*, 17, 429.

Chesney, K. (1972), *The Victorian Underworld* (Harmondsworth: Pelican).

Chesterman, M.R. (1984), 'Family Settlements on Trust: Landowners and the Rising Bourgeoisie', in Rubin, G. and Sugarman, D. (eds), *Law, Economy and Society* (Abingdon: Professional Books).

Clark J.C.D. (1982), *The Dynamics of Change, the Crisis of the 1750s and the English Party System* (Cambridge University Press).

Clark, J.C.D. (1985), *English Society 1688–1832* (Cambridge University Press).

Close, P. and Collins, R. (eds) (1985), *Family and Economy in Modern Society* (London: Macmillan).

Cobbett, William, *Parliamentary History*, vols. IX, XIV and XV.

Cockburn, C. (1978), *The Local State* (London: Pluto Press).

Cohen, S. (1980), *Folk Devils and Moral Panics* (Oxford: Martin Robertson).

Coleman, T. (1965), *The Railway Navvies* (London: Hutchinson).

Colwell, S. (1980), 'The Incidence of Bigamy in Eighteenth and Nineteenth Century England', *Family History*, 91.

Corby, B. (1987), *Working with Child Abuse* (Milton Keynes: Open University Press).

Coward, J. (1987), 'Conceptions outside Marriage: Regional Differences', *Population Trends*, 49 (London: HMSO).

Cox, J.C. (1910), *The Parish Registers of England* (London).

Cretney, S.M. (1980), 'The Law Relating to Unmarried Partners from the Perspective of a Law Reform Agency', in Eekelaar, J.M. and Katz, S.N. (eds), *Marriage and Cohabitation in Contemporary Societies* (London: Butterworths).

Cretney, S.M. (1984), *Principles of Family Law* (London: Sweet & Maxwell).

Cretney, S.M. (1986), 'Money after Divorce—the Mistakes we have Made?', in Freeman, M.D.A., *Essays in Family Law 1985* (London: Stevens).

Cretney, S.M. (1987), *Elements of Family Law* (London: Butterworths).

Dale, J. and Foster, P. (1986), *Feminists and State Welfare* (London: Routledge & Kegan Paul).

David, M.E. (1980), *The State, the Family and Education* (London: Routledge & Kegan Paul).

Davidoff, L. (1983), 'Class and Gender in Victorian England', in Newton, J.L. *et al.* (eds), *Sex and Class in Women's History* (London: Routledge & Kegan Paul).

Deech, R. (1986), 'The Work of the Law Commission in Family Law: The First Twenty Years', in Freeman, M.D.A., *Essays in Family Law 1985* (London: Stevens).

Delamont, S. (1980), *The Sociology of Women* (London: Allen & Unwin).

Denning, Lord (1980), *The Due Process of Law* (London: Butterworths).

Devlin, P. (1965), *The Enforcement of Morals* (Oxford University Press).

Dingwall, R., Eekelaar, J.M. and Murray, T. (1983), *The Protection of Children* (Oxford: Blackwell).

Dingwall, R. and Eekelaar, J.M. (eds) (1988), *Divorce Mediation and the Legal Process* (Oxford: Clarendon Press).

Donajgrodzki, A.P. (1977), *Social Control in Nineteenth Century Britain* (London: Croom Helm).

Donzelot, J. (1980), *The Policing of Families* (London: Hutchinson).

Duncan, W.R. (1978), 'Supporting the Institution of Marriage in Ireland', *The Irish Jurist*, 215.

Dunnell, K. (1979), *Family Formation Survey* (London: HMSO).

Dyer, C. and Berlins, M. (1982), *Living Together* (London: Hamlyn).

Edwards, S.S.M. and Halpern, A. (1987), 'Financial Provision, Case-law and Statistical Trends since 1984', *Family Law*, 17, 354.

Edwards, S.S.M. and Halpern, A. (1988), 'Maintenance in 1987: Fact or Fantasy?', *Family Law*, 18, 117.

Eekelaar, J.M. (1971), *Family Security and Family Breakdown* (Harmondsworth: Penguin).

Eekelaar, J.M. (1978), *Family Law and Social Policy*, 1st edn (London: Weidenfeld & Nicolson).

Eekelaar, J.M. (1980), 'Crisis in the Institution of Marriage: An Overview', in Eekelaar, J.M. and Katz, S.N. (eds), *Marriage and Cohabitation in Contemporary Societies* (London: Butterworths).

Eekelaar, J.M. 1984), *Family Law and Social Policy*, 2nd edn (London: Weidenfeld & Nicolson).

Eekelaar, J.M. and MacLean, S. (1986), *Maintenance after Divorce* (Oxford: Clarendon Press).

Elliott, F.R. (1986), *The Family: Change or Continuity?* (London: Macmillan).

Ellis, H. (1937), *Sex in Relation to Society*, originally published as *Studies in the Psychology of Sex* (London: Heinemann).

Equal Opportunities Commission (1986), *Women and Men in Britain* (London: HMSO).

Fairbairns, Z. (1985), 'The Cohabitation Rule—Why it makes Sense', in Ungerson, C. (ed.), *Women and Social Policy* (London: Macmillan).

Feinstein, C.H. (1981), 'Capital Accumulation and the Industrial Revolution', in Floud, R. and McCloskey, D. (eds), *The Economic History of Britain since 1700* (Cambridge University Press).

Fielding, W.J. (1961), *Strange Customs of Courtship and Marriage* (London: Souvenir Press).

Finer, M. (1974), *Report on One-Parent Families* (London: HMSO).

Finer, S.E. (1952), *The Life and Times of Sir Edwin Chadwick* (London: Methuen).

Floud, R. and Thane, P. (1979), 'The Incidence of Civil Marriage in Victorian England and Wales', *Past and Present*, 84, 146.

Forster, E.M. (1956), *Marianne Thornton, a Domestic Biography 1797–1897* (New York).

Fowles, J. (1969), *The French Lieutenant's Woman* (London: Jonathan Cape).

Freeman, M.D.A. (1979), *Violence in the Home* (Farnborough: Saxon House).

Freeman, M.D.A. (1981), 'The State, the Family and the Law in the Eighties', *Kingston Law Review*, 11, 130.

Freeman M.D.A. (1984a), *State, Law and Family* (London: Tavistock).

Freeman, M.D.A. (1984b), 'Legal Ideologies, Patriarchal Precedents and Domestic Violence', in Freeman (1984a).

Freeman, M.D.A. (1984c), 'Family Matters', in Jowell, J.L. and McAuslan, J.P.W.B. (eds), *Lord Denning, the Judge and the Law* (London: Sweet & Maxwell).

Freeman, M.D.A. (1986), *Essays in Family Law 1985* (London: Stevens).

Freeman, M.D.A. and Lyon, C.M. (1983), *Cohabitation without Marriage* (Aldershot: Gower).

Geddes, P. and Thompson, J.A. (1914), *Sex* (London).

General Household Survey (1979), (London: HMSO).
General Household Survey (1980), (London: HMSO).
General Household Survey (1984), (London: HMSO).
Gill, D. (1977), *Illegitimacy, Sexuality and the Status of Women* (Oxford: Blackwell).
Gillis, J.R. (1974), *Youth and History: Traditions and Changes in European Age Relations 1770–Present* (London: Academic Press).
Gillis, J.R. (1980), 'Resort to Common Law Marriage in England and Wales 1700–1850', unpublished paper presented to 1980 *Past and Present* Conference on Law and Human Relations.
Gillis, J.R. (1985), *For Better, for Worse. British Marriages 1600 to the Present* (Oxford University Press).
Ginsburg, N. (1979), *Class, Capital and Social Policy* (London, Macmillan).
Gittins, D. (1985), *The Family in Question* (London: Macmillan).
Glendon, M.A. (1977), *State, Law and Family* (Oxford: North-Holland).
Glendon, M.A. (1981), *The New Family and the New Property* (London, Butterworths).
Golby, J.M. and Purdue, A.W. (1984), *The Civilization of the Crowd: Popular Culture in England 1750–1900* (London: Batsford).
Goody, J. (1983), *The Development of the Family and Marriage in Europe* (Cambridge University Press).
Gorer, G. (1960), *Exploring English Character* (London: Cressnet Press).
Gorer, G. (1971), *Sex and Marriage in England Today* (London: Nelson).
Gough, I. (1979), *The Political Economy of the Welfare State* (London: Macmillan).
Gray, R. (1977), 'Bourgeois Hegemony in Victorian Britain', in Bloomfield, J. (ed.), *Class, Hegemony and Party* (London: Lawrence & Wishart).
Greenwood, V. and Young, J. (eds) (1980), *Permissiveness and Control* (London: Hutchinson).
Gwyn, G. (1928), *Folklore.*
Hall, C. (1982), 'The Home Turned Upside Down? The Working Class Family in Cotton Textiles 1780–1850', in Whitelegg, E. (ed.), *The Changing Experience of Women* (Oxford: Martin Robertson).
Hall, S. (1978), *Policing the Crisis* (London: Macmillan).
Hall, S. (1979), *Drifting into a Law and Order Society* (London: Cobden Trust).
Hall, S. (1980), 'Reformism and the Legislation of Consent', in Greenwood, V. and Young, J. (eds), *Permissiveness and Control* (London: Hutchinson).
Hardy, T. (1960), *Tess of the D'Urbervilles* (London: Macmillan).
Hardy, T. (1975), *The Well-Beloved* (London: Macmillan).
Harrison, J.F.C. (1979), *Early Victorian Britain* (London: Fontana).
Harrison, R. and Mort, F. (1980), 'Patriarchal Aspects of Nineteenth Century State Formation: Property Relations, Marriage and Divorce, and Sexuality', in Corrigan, P. (ed.), *Capitalism, State Formation and Marxist Theory* (London: Quartet).
Haskey, J. (1985), 'Cohabitation before Marriage: a Comparison of Information from Marriage Registration and the General Household Survey', *Population Trends* 39 (London: HMSO).

Haskey, J. (1987a), 'Social Class Differentials in Remarriage and Divorce: Results from a Forward Linkage Study', *Population Trends* 47 (London: HMSO).

Haskey, J. (1987b), 'Trends in Marriage and Divorce in England and Wales: 1837–1987', *Population Trends* 48 (London: HMSO).

Haw, R. (1952), *The State of Matrimony* (London: SPCK).

Hay, D. (1977), 'Poaching and the Game Laws on Cannock Chase', in Hay, D. *et al.* (eds), *Albion's Fatal Tree* (Harmondsworth: Peregrine).

Helmholz, R.M. (1974), *Marriage Litigation in Medieval England* (Cambridge University Press).

Hill, C. (1975), *The World Turned Upside Down* (Harmondsworth: Penguin).

Hirst, P. (1980), 'The Genesis of the Social', in *Politics and Power 3* (London: Routledge & Kegan Paul).

Hobsbawm, E.J. (1964), *Labouring Men: Studies in the History of Labour* (London: Weidenfeld & Nicolson).

Hobsbawm, E.J. (1969), *Industry and Empire* (Harmondsworth: Penguin).

Hoggett, B. (1982), 'Families and the Law', in Rapoport R.N. *et al.* (eds), *Families in Britain* (London: Routledge & Kegan Paul).

Hoggett, B. and Pearl, D. (1983), *The Family, Law and Society* 1st edn (London: Butterworths).

Hoggett, B. and Pearl, D. (1987), *The Family, Law and Society*, 2nd edn (London: Butterworths).

Holcombe, L. (1983), *Wives and Property* (Oxford: Martin Robertson).

Holdsworth, Sir W. *A History of English Law*, xi (London).

Horn, P. (1980), *The Rural World 1780–1850: Social Change in the English Countryside* (London: Hutchinson).

Houlbrooke, R. (1979), *Church Courts and the People During the English Reformation 1520–1570* (Oxford University Press).

Houlbrooke, R. (1984), *The English Family 1450–1700* (London: Longman).

Howard, G.E. (1904), *A History of Matrimonial Institutions* (University of Chicago Press).

Humphries, J. (1977), 'The Working Class Family', *Review of Radical Political Economy*, 9, 25.

Ifan, D. (1972), *Cereidigion*, viii, 201.

Ingram, M. (1980), 'Spousals Litigation in the English Ecclesiastical Courts *c.* 1350–*c.* 1640', in Outhwaite, R.B. (ed.), *Marriage and Society* (London, Europa).

Jackson, J. (1969), *Formation and Annulment of Marriage* (London: Butterworths).

Jarrett, D. (1976), *England in the Age of Hogarth* (St Albans: Paladin).

Johnson, R.W. (1976), 'Barrington Moore, Perry Anderson and English Social Development', *Working Papers in Cultural Studies*, 9, 24.

Jones, C. and Novak, T. (1980), 'The State and Social Policy', in Corrigan, P. (ed.), *Capitalism, State Formation and Marxist Theory* (London: Quartet).

Jones, T.G. (1930), *Welsh Folklore and Folk-Custom* (republished 1979, Cardiff: Brewer).

Kahn-Freund, O. and Wedderburn, C.W. (1971), foreword to Eekelaar,

J.M. *Family Security and Family Breakdown* (Harmondsworth: Penguin).

Kidd, T. (1982), 'Social Security and the Family', in Reid, I. and Wormald, E. (eds), *Sex Differences in Britain* (London: Grant MacIntyre).

Land, H. (1984), 'Changing Women's Claims to Maintenance', in Freeman, M.D.A., *State, Law and Family* (London: Tavistock).

Lasch, C. (1974), 'The Suppression of Clandestine Marriage in England; the Marriage Act of 1753', *Salmagundi*, 90.

Laslett, P. (1977), *Family Life and Illicit Love in Earlier Generations* (Cambridge University Press).

Laslett, P. (1980), *Bastardy and its Comparative History* (London: Edward Arnold).

Laslett, P. (1982), foreword to Rappoport, R.N. *et al.* (eds), *Families in Britain* (London: Routledge & Kegan Paul).

Lecky, W.E.H. (1883), *A History of England in the Eighteenth Century* (London).

Leonard, D. (1980), *Sex and Generation* (London: Tavistock).

Levine, D. (1977), *Family Formation in an Age of Nascent Capitalism* (London: Academic Press).

Lewis, J. (1980), *The Politics of Motherhood. Child and Maternal Welfare in England 1900–1939* (London: Croom Helm).

Lewis, J. (1983), *Women's Welfare, Women's Rights* (London: Croom Helm).

McCann, K. (1985), 'Battered Women and the Law: the Limits of the Legislation', in Brophy, J. and Smart, C. (eds), *Women in Law* (London: Routledge & Kegan Paul).

McCulloch, A. (1982), 'Alternative Households', in Rappoport, R.N. *et al.* (eds), *Families in Britain* (London: Routledge & Kegan Paul).

Macfarlane, A. (1978), *The Origins of English Individualism* (Oxford: Blackwell).

Macfarlane, A. (1980), 'Illegitimacy and Illegitimates in English History', in Laslett, P. (ed.), *Bastardy and its Comparative History* (London: Edward Arnold).

Macfarlane, A. (1986), *Marriage and Love in England, Modes of Reproduction 1300–1840* (Oxford: Blackwell).

McIntosh, M. (1978), 'The Welfare State and the Needs of the Dependent Family', in Littlejohn, G. *et al.* (eds), *Power and the State* (London: Croom Helm).

McMurtry, J. (1972), 'Monogamy', *The Monist*, 56, 592.

MacQueen, J.F. (1858), *Divorce and Matrimonial Jurisdictions* (Edinburgh).

Mahon, Lord (1858), *The History of England 1713–1780* (London).

Malcolmson, R.W. (1981), *Life and Labour in England 1700–1780* (London: Hutchinson).

Manchester, A.H. (1980), *Modern Legal History* (London: Butterworths).

Marriage and Divorce Statistics 1985 (1987), (London: HMSO).

Marwick, A. (1982), *British Society since 1945* (Harmondsworth: Penguin).

Mayhew, H. (1861), *London Labour and London Poor* (London).

Medick, H. (1976), 'The Proto-Industrial Family Economy: the Structural Function of Household and Family during the Transition from Peasant Society to Industrial Capitalism', *Social History*, 3, 291.

Menefee, S.P. (1981), *Wives for Sale* (Oxford: Blackwell).

Meteyard, B. (1980), 'Illegitimacy and Marriage in Eighteenth Century England', *Journal of Interdisciplinary History*, 3, 479.

Monitor (1981), (London: HMSO).

Morgan, D.W.J. (1985), *The Family, Politics and Social Theory* (London: Routledge & Kegan Paul).

Morris, R.J. (1979), *Class and Class Consciousness in the Industrial Revolution* (London: Macmillan).

Mueller, G.O.W. (1957), 'Inquiry into the State of a Divorceless Society', *University of Pittsburgh Law Review*, 18, 545.

Murch, M. (1980), *Justice and Welfare in Divorce* (London: Sweet & Maxwell).

Newman, A. (1980), 'An Evaluation of Bastardy Recordings in an East Kent Parish', in Laslett, P. (ed.), *Bastardy and Its Comparative History* (London: Edward Arnold).

Oakley, A. (1982), 'Conventional Families', in Rappoport, R. *et al.* (eds), *Families in Britain* (London: Routledge & Kegan Paul).

O'Donovan, K. (1985), *Sexual Divisions in Law* (London: Weidenfeld & Nicolson).

Oliver, D. (1982), 'Why do People Live Together?', *Journal of Social Welfare Law*, 209.

Oliver, D. (1987), *Cohabitation: The Legal Implications* (London: Commerce Clearing House).

Outhwaite, R.B. (1973), 'Age of Marriage in England from the late Seventeenth to the late Nineteenth Centuries', *Transactions of the Royal Historical Society*, 5th series, xvii, 64.

Outhwaite, R.B. (1980), *Marriage and Society: Studies in the Social History of Marriage* (London: Europa).

Pahl, J. (1980), 'Patterns of Money Management within Marriage', *Journal of Social Policy*, 313.

Pahl, J. (1984), 'The Allocation of Money within the Household', in Freeman, M.D.A., *State, Law and Family* (London: Tavistock).

Pahl, J. (ed.) (1985), *Private Violence and Public Policy* (London: Routledge & Kegan Paul).

Parker, S. (1981), *Cohabitees* (Chichester: Barry Rose).

Parker, S. (1984), 'Unmarried Cohabitation: A Threat to the Patriarchal Family?', *Contemporary Crises*, 8, 175.

Parker, S. (1985a), *Legal Responses to Informal Marriage and Cohabitation since 1750*, PhD thesis, University of Wales.

Parker, S. (1985b), 'The Legal Background', in Pahl, J. (ed.), *Private Violence and Public Policy* (London: Routledge & Kegan Paul).

Parker, S. (1987), *Cohabitees*, 2nd edn (London: Kluwer).

Parkinson, L. (1988), 'Child Custody Orders: A Legal Lottery', *Family Law*, 18, 27.

Parry, M.L. (1981), *Cohabitation* (London: Sweet & Maxwell).

Pascall, G. (1986), *Social Policy: A Feminist Critique* (London: Tavistock).

Pinchbeck, I. (1930), *Women Workers and the Industrial Revolution 1750–1850* (London: Routledge).

Plucknett, T.F.T. (1940), *A Concise History of the Common Law* (London: Butterworths).

Population Trends 14 (1978), (London: HMSO).

Population Trends 51 (1988), (London: HMSO).

Porter, R. (1982), *English Society in the Eighteenth Century* (Harmondsworth: Penguin).

Poster, M. (1978), *Critical Theory of the Family* (London: Pluto Press).

Poynter, J.R. (1969), *Society and Pauperism: English Ideas on Poor Relief, 1795–1834* (London: Routledge & Kegan Paul).

Price, S. (1979), 'Ideologies of Female Dependence in the Welfare State— Women's Response to the Beveridge Report', paper presented to the 1979 British Sociological Association Conference on Law and Society.

Pryce, H. and Jones, J.G. (1984), 'Articles relating to the History of Wales', *Welsh History Review*, 12, 295.

Pryce, W.T.R. (1978–80), 'Welsh and English in Wales 1750–1971', *Board of Celtic Studies Bulletin*, 28, 26.

Quaife, G.R. (1979), *Wanton Wives and Wayward Wenches: Peasants and Illicit Sex in early Seventeenth Century England* (London: Croom Helm).

Redford, A. (1926), *Labour Migration in England 1800–50* (Manchester University Press).

Rees, A. (1975), *Life in a Welsh Countryside* (Cardiff: University of Wales Press).

Reich, C. (1964), 'The New Property', *Yale Law Journal*, 73, 773.

Reid, I. (1981), *Social Class Differences in Britain* (London: Grant MacIntyre).

Rheinstein, M. (1972), *Marriage Stability, Divorce and the Law* (University of Chicago Press).

Rhys, J. (1901), *Celtic Folklore, Welsh and Manx*.

Richards, P. (1980), 'State Formation and Class Struggle 1832–48', in Corrigan, P. (ed.), *Capitalism, State Formation and Marxist Theory* (London: Quartet).

Richards, M.P.M. (1987), 'Children, Parents and Families: Developmental Psychology and the Re-Ordering of Relationships at Divorce', *International Journal of Family Law*, 1, 295.

Rimmer, L. (1981), *Families in Focus* (London: Study Commission on the Family).

Roberts, R. (1973), *The Classic Slum* (Harmondsworth: Pelican).

Robertson, Sir C. (1911), *England under the Hanoverians* (London: Methuen).

Rose, M.E. (1981), 'Social Change and the Industrial Revolution', in Floud, R. and McCloskey, D. (eds), *The Economic History of Britain since 1750* (Cambridge University Press).

Royal Commission into the Operation and Administration of the Poor Law (1834) (London).

Royal Commission Appointed to Inquire into the State and Operation of the Law of Marriage as Relating to the Prohibited Degrees of Affinity (1847–8) (London).

Royal Commission on the Laws of Marriage (1868).

Royal Commission on Marriage and Divorce (1956) (London: HMSO).

Rubin, G.R. and Sugarman, D. (eds) (1984), *Law, Economy and Society, Essays in the History of English Law 1750–1914* (Abingdon: Professional Books).

Rule, J.S. (1982), 'Methodism, Popular Beliefs and Village Culture in Cornwall 1800–1850', in Storch, R.D. (ed.), *Popular Culture and Custom in Nineteenth Century England* (London: Croom Helm).

Scheingold, S. (1988), 'Radical Lawyers and Socialist Ideals', *Journal of Law and Society*, 15, 122.

Scott, J. and Tilly, L. (1975), 'Women's Work and the Family in Nineteenth Century Europe', *Comparative Studies in Society and History*, XVII, 42.

Shebbeare, J. (1974), *The Marriage Act* (Garland).

Shorter, E. (1977), *The Making of the Modern Family* (London: Fontana).

Simpson, J. (1976), *The Folk-Lore of the Welsh Borders* (London: Batsford).

Smart, C. (1982), 'Regulating Families or Legitimating Patriarchy? Family Law in Britain', *International Journal of Sociology of Law*, 10, 129.

Smart, C. (1984), *The Ties that Bind: Law, Marriage and the Production of Patriarchal Relations* (London: Routledge & Kegan Paul).

Smart, C. (1984b), 'Marriage, Divorce and Women's Economic Dependency', in Freeman, M.D.A., *State, Law and Family* (London: Tavistock).

Smollett, T. (1830), *The History of England* (London).

Smout, T.C. (1981), 'Scottish Marriage, Regular and Irregular 1500–1940', in Outhwaite, R.B., *Marriage and Society* (London: Europa).

Social Trends 10 (1979) (London: HMSO).

Social Trends 15 (1985) (London: HMSO).

Social Trends 17 (1987) (London: HMSO).

Social Trends 18 (1988) (London: HMSO).

Spring, E. (1984), 'The Family, Strict Settlement and Historians', in Rubin, G. and Sugarman, D. (eds), *Law, Economy and Society* (Abingdon: Professional Books).

Stetson, D.M. (1982), *A Woman's Issue* (London: Greenwood Press).

Stone, L. (1979), *The Family, Sex and Marriage in England 1500–1800* (Harmondsworth: Penguin).

Stone, L. and Stone, J.C. Fawtier (1984), *An Open Elite? England 1540–1880* (Oxford: Clarendon Press).

Stone, O. (1977), *Family Law* (London: Macmillan).

Storch, R.D. (1977), 'The Problem of Working-Class Leisure. Some Roots of middle-class Moral Reform in the Industrial North 1825–50', in Donajgrodzki, A.P. (ed.), *Social Control in Nineteenth Century Britain* (London: Croom Helm).

Storch, R.D. (1982), *Popular Culture and Custom in Nineteenth Century England* (London: Croom Helm).

Taylor-Gooby, P. and Dale, J. (1981), *Social Theory and Social Welfare* (London: Edward Arnold).

Thompson, E.P. (1968), *The Making of the English Working Class* (Harmondsworth: Pelican).

Thompson, E.P. (1977), *Whigs and Hunters* (Harmondsworth: Peregrine).

Thompson, E.P. (1978), 'The Peculiarities of the English', in *The Poverty of Theory* (London: Merlin).

Tillotson, K. (1954), *Novels of the 1840s* (Oxford University Press).

Tilly, L.A. and Scott, J.W. (1978), *Women, Work and Family* (New York: Holt, Rhinehart & Winston).

Tolson, A. (1975), *The Family in a 'Permissive Society'* (University of Birmingham).

Torr, D. (1956), *Tom Mann and his Times* (London: Lawrence & Wishart).
Tranter, N.L. (1981), 'The Labour Supply 1780–1860', in Floud, R. and McCloskey, D. (eds), *The Economic History of Britain since 1700* (Cambridge University Press).
Trevelyan, G.O. (1881), *The Early History of Charles James Fox* (London).
Trumbach, R. (1978), *The Rise of the Egalitarian Family* (London: Academic Press).
Tyerman, L. (1870), *John Wesley* (London).
Villiers (1833) Report in *Extracts from the Information Received by HM Commissioners as to the Operation of the Poor Laws* (London).
Walpole, H. (1847), *Memoirs of the Reign of King George the Second* (London).
Webb, M. (1982), *The Labour Market*, in Reid, I. and Wormald, E. (eds), *Sex Differences in Britain* (London: Grant MacIntyre).
Webb, J.S. (1988), 'Maintenance Payments, Social Security and the Liable Relative: (1) Supplementary Benefit', *Family Law*, 18, 267.
Weber, A.F. (1899), *The Growth of Cities in the Nineteenth Century* (New York).
Weber, M. (1964), *The Theory of Social and Economic Organisation* (New York: Free Press).
Weeks, J. (1981), *Sex Politics and Society* (London: Longman).
Williams, R. (1976), *Keywords* (London: Fontana).
Williams, R. (1980), *Problems in Materialism and Culture* (London: Verso).
Williams, W. (1908), *Itinerary through Wales* (London).
Willmot, P. and Young, M. (1957), *Family and Kinship in East London* (London: Routledge & Kegan Paul).
Willmot, P. and Young, M. (1960), *Family and Class in a London Suburb* (London: Routledge & Kegan Paul).
Wilson, E. (1977), *Women and the Welfare State* (London: Tavistock).
Wolfram, S. (1987), *In-Laws and Outlaws: Kinship and Marriage in England* (London: Croom Helm).
Wood, G.A. (1975), 'Church and State in New Zealand in the 1850s', *Journal of Religious History*, 8, 225.
Worsley-Boden (1932), *Mischiefs of the Marriage Law* (Williams & Norgate).
Wrigley, E.A. (1973), 'Clandestine Marriage in Tetbury in the late 17th Century', *Local Population Studies*, 15.
Wynne, J. (1955), 'A Report on the Deanry of Penllyn and Edeirnian, 1730', *The Merioneth Miscellany*, 8.
Zaretsky, E. (1976), *Capitalism, the Family and Personal Life* (London: Pluto Press).

Index

174